TEACHER'S PET PUBLICATIONS

PUZZLE PACK
for
The Pinballs

based on the book by
Betsy Byars

Written by
William T. Collins

© 2005 Teacher's Pet Publications
All Rights Reserved

The materials in this packet are copyrighted
by Teacher's Pet Publications, Inc.

These pages may be duplicated by the purchaser
for use in the purchaser's own classroom.

Copying any of these materials and distributing them
for any other purpose is a violation of the copyright laws.

© 2005 Teacher's Pet Publications, Inc.
www.tpet.com

INTRODUCTION
If you already own the LitPlan for this title, this Puzzle Pack will refresh your Unit Resource Materials and Vocabulary Resource Materials sections plus give you additional materials you can substitute into the tests.If you do not already have a complete LitPlan, these pages will give you some supplemental materials to use with your own plan. There are two main groups of materials: one set for unit words (such as characters' names, symbols, places, etc.) and one set for vocabulary words associated with the book.

WORD LIST
There is a word list for both the unit words and the vocabulary words. These lists show you which words are being used in the materials and the clues or definitions being used for those words. You may want to give students a word list with clues/definitions to help them, or you may want students to only have a word list (without clues/definitions) if you want them to work a little harder. Both are available for duplication. The word lists can also be your "calling key" for the bingo games.

FILL IN THE BLANK AND MATCHING
There are 4 each of the fill in the blank and matching worksheets for both the unit and vocabulary words. These pages can be used either as extra worksheets for students or as objective parts of a unit test. They can be done individually if students need extra help or as a whole class activity to review the material covered.

MAGIC SQUARES
The magic squares not only reinforce the material covered but also work on reasoning and math skills. Many teachers have told us that their students really enjoy doing these!

WORD SEARCH PUZZLES
The word search words go in all directions, as indicated on your answer keys. Two of the word search puzzles have the clues listed rather than the words. This makes the puzzle a little more difficult, but it reinforces the material better. Two word search puzzles have words only for students who find the clue puzzles too difficult.

CROSSWORD PUZZLES
Both unit and vocabulary word sections have 4 crossword puzzles.

BINGO CARDS
There are 32 individual bingo cards for the unit words and 32 individual bingo cards for the vocabulary words. You can use your word list as a "call list," calling the words at random and marking them off of your list as you go, or you could use the flash cards by cutting them apart and drawing the words at random from a hat (or box or whatever). To make a better review, you might ask for the definition and spelling of each word as you call it out–or you could call out the definitions and have students tell you the words they need to look for on the puzzle.

JUGGLE LETTERS
The vocabulary juggle letter game is intended to help students learn the spellings of the words. One sheet has the definitions listed on it as an extra help for students who need it or to reinforce the definitions if you choose to do so.

FLASH CARDS
We've included a set of vocabulary flash cards you can duplicate, cut, and fold for your students. Some teachers make a few sets for general use by the class; others make a set for each student. Some teachers duplicate them for each student and have the students cut & fold their own. You can cut out just the words and put them in a hat, have each student pick out one word and write the definition and a sentence for that word. Students then swap words and papers, with the next student adding a sentence of his own under the last one. You can have students swap as many times as you like. Each time the student will read the sentences written prior to his own and then add a sentence. You can cut out the words and definitions separately and play "I Have; Who Has?" Each student in the room draws a word and definition. The first student says, "I have (the name of the word). Who has the definition?" The student with the definition reads it then says, "I have (the name of the vocabulary word she has). Who has the definition?" The round continues until all words and definitions have been given.

Pinballs Unit Word List

No.	Word	Clue/Definition
1.	AUGUST	Month of birthday for Carlie and Thomas J
2.	BARBER	Where Thomas J went for a real haircut
3.	BETHENIA	Harvey's mother's new name at the commune
4.	BIBLE	Book Benson twins gave Thomas J; Big ___ Stories
5.	BYARS	Author
6.	CAMEO	Benson twins' jewelry
7.	CANDY	Benson twins don't believe in it
8.	CARLIE	Teenage girl sent to foster home
9.	CASKET	Mr. Mason told Thomas J about bumping Mr. Joe's ___
10.	CASTS	Harvey has two of these
11.	CHER	Carlie's favorite stars; Sonny and ___
12.	COINS	Gift from twins to Thomas J; gold ___
13.	CONSTRUCTION	Business of Harvey's dad
14.	DAWN	Benson twins' favorite TV show; Tony Orlando & ___
15.	DECALS	Carlie wanted to put them on Harvey's toes
16.	DECORETTES	Silver cake decorations
17.	DYING	Carlie's Number One Rule as a nurse; No ___
18.	EARRING	Carlie lost this & Thomas J found it
19.	ELKS	Place Harvey's dad wanted to go
20.	ERASER	What Carlie wants to use on the bad memories
21.	FOOTBALL	How Harvey explains his broken legs; ___ injury
22.	FUNERALS	Where Thomas J went with Mr. Mason
23.	GRANDAM	Harvey's dad's car
24.	HALTERS	Carlie learned to sew these
25.	HAMMOCK	Picture in article shows Harvey's mom making one
26.	HARVEY	Boy with two legs in casts
27.	JEFFERSON	First twin to die; ___ Benson
28.	KFC	Food to which Harvey was addicted
29.	LETTER	What Carlie hoped would come from her mother
30.	LIBRARY	Where Carlie takes Harvey in his wheelchair
31.	LISTS	Harvey made these and learned about himself
32.	MAJORETTE	Carlie couldn't be one due to bad grades
33.	MARTINIS	Harvey's father drank these to forget
34.	MASON	Carlie, Thomas J, & Harvey's foster mother; Mrs. ___
35.	MAYONNAISE	Carlie's famous dessert for Harvey; ___ cake
36.	MOSES	Thomas J's favorite bible story; Baby ___
37.	NURSE	Vocation Carlie has chosen; Good Luck ___
38.	PINBALL	Carlie compares one to her life; ___ machine
39.	PINBALLS	Carlie says they have no control over themselves
40.	PUPPY	Gift Thomas J and Carlie gave Harvey
41.	RESTLESS	Carlie's favorite show; Young and The ___
42.	SHOUTED	How Thomas J spoke
43.	SNOOPY	Thomas wore a ___ t-shirt when dropped off
44.	SNOWBALL	Harvey's guinea pig
45.	THOMAS	Second twin to die
46.	TIMES	Had article about Harvey's mother; New York ___
47.	TV	Harvey's birthday present
48.	TWO	Number of stepfathers Carlie has
49.	VIRGINIA	Where Harvey's mother makes hammocks
50.	WORM	Funny present for Harvey's puppy; ___ pills
51.	XEROX	Harvey's copy of his mother's article
52.	YOGA	Classes Harvey's mother took

Pinballs Fill In The Blank 1

_____ 1. Carlie learned to sew these

_____ 2. Silver cake decorations

_____ 3. Harvey has two of these

_____ 4. Carlie's favorite stars; Sonny and _____

_____ 5. Carlie, Thomas J, & Harvey's foster mother; Mrs. ___

_____ 6. How Harvey explains his broken legs; ___ injury

_____ 7. Classes Harvey's mother took

_____ 8. Carlie couldn't be one due to bad grades

_____ 9. Carlie lost this & Thomas J found it

_____ 10. Harvey's birthday present

_____ 11. Carlie's favorite show; Young and The ___

_____ 12. Month of birthday for Carlie and Thomas J

_____ 13. Where Thomas J went with Mr. Mason

_____ 14. Number of stepfathers Carlie has

_____ 15. Carlie's Number One Rule as a nurse; No ___

_____ 16. Gift from twins to Thomas J; gold ___

_____ 17. Mr. Mason told Thomas J about bumping Mr. Joe's ____

_____ 18. Place Harvey's dad wanted to go

_____ 19. Carlie says they have no control over themselves

_____ 20. Carlie's famous dessert for Harvey; ___ cake

Pinballs Fill In The Blank 1 Answer Key

HALTERS	1. Carlie learned to sew these
DECORETTES	2. Silver cake decorations
CASTS	3. Harvey has two of these
CHER	4. Carlie's favorite stars; Sonny and _____
MASON	5. Carlie, Thomas J, & Harvey's foster mother; Mrs. ___
FOOTBALL	6. How Harvey explains his broken legs; ___ injury
YOGA	7. Classes Harvey's mother took
MAJORETTE	8. Carlie couldn't be one due to bad grades
EARRING	9. Carlie lost this & Thomas J found it
TV	10. Harvey's birthday present
RESTLESS	11. Carlie's favorite show; Young and The ___
AUGUST	12. Month of birthday for Carlie and Thomas J
FUNERALS	13. Where Thomas J went with Mr. Mason
TWO	14. Number of stepfathers Carlie has
DYING	15. Carlie's Number One Rule as a nurse; No ___
COINS	16. Gift from twins to Thomas J; gold ___
CASKET	17. Mr. Mason told Thomas J about bumping Mr. Joe's ____
ELKS	18. Place Harvey's dad wanted to go
PINBALLS	19. Carlie says they have no control over themselves
MAYONNAISE	20. Carlie's famous dessert for Harvey; ___ cake

Pinballs Fill In The Blank 2

1. Carlie lost this & Thomas J found it
2. Thomas J's favorite bible story; Baby ___
3. Place Harvey's dad wanted to go
4. Harvey made these and learned about himself
5. Where Thomas J went for a real haircut
6. Carlie says they have no control over themselves
7. Carlie compares one to her life; ___ machine
8. Harvey's father drank these to forget
9. Where Thomas J went with Mr. Mason
10. What Carlie wants to use on the bad memories
11. Harvey's birthday present
12. Harvey's dad's car
13. Picture in article shows Harvey's mom making one
14. Harvey has two of these
15. Carlie's favorite stars; Sonny and _____
16. Carlie, Thomas J, & Harvey's foster mother; Mrs. ___
17. How Thomas J spoke
18. Number of stepfathers Carlie has
19. Thomas wore a ___ t-shirt when dropped off
20. Book Benson twins gave Thomas J; Big ___ Stories

Pinballs Fill In The Blank 2 Answer Key

EARRING	1. Carlie lost this & Thomas J found it
MOSES	2. Thomas J's favorite bible story; Baby ___
ELKS	3. Place Harvey's dad wanted to go
LISTS	4. Harvey made these and learned about himself
BARBER	5. Where Thomas J went for a real haircut
PINBALLS	6. Carlie says they have no control over themselves
PINBALL	7. Carlie compares one to her life; ___ machine
MARTINIS	8. Harvey's father drank these to forget
FUNERALS	9. Where Thomas J went with Mr. Mason
ERASER	10. What Carlie wants to use on the bad memories
TV	11. Harvey's birthday present
GRANDAM	12. Harvey's dad's car
HAMMOCK	13. Picture in article shows Harvey's mom making one
CASTS	14. Harvey has two of these
CHER	15. Carlie's favorite stars; Sonny and _____
MASON	16. Carlie, Thomas J, & Harvey's foster mother; Mrs. ___
SHOUTED	17. How Thomas J spoke
TWO	18. Number of stepfathers Carlie has
SNOOPY	19. Thomas wore a ___ t-shirt when dropped off
BIBLE	20. Book Benson twins gave Thomas J; Big ___ Stories

Pinballs Fill In The Blank 3

1. Funny present for Harvey's puppy; ____ pills
2. Benson twins' jewelry
3. Second twin to die
4. Had article about Harvey's mother; New York ___
5. Author
6. Teenage girl sent to foster home
7. Carlie's Number One Rule as a nurse; No ___
8. Carlie's favorite stars; Sonny and _____
9. How Harvey explains his broken legs; ___ injury
10. Where Thomas J went with Mr. Mason
11. Gift Thomas J and Carlie gave Harvey
12. Carlie learned to sew these
13. Gift from twins to Thomas J; gold ___
14. Month of birthday for Carlie and Thomas J
15. Thomas wore a ___ t-shirt when dropped off
16. What Carlie hoped would come from her mother
17. Where Thomas J went for a real haircut
18. Classes Harvey's mother took
19. What Carlie wants to use on the bad memories
20. Boy with two legs in casts

Pinballs Fill In The Blank 3 Answer Key

WORM	1. Funny present for Harvey's puppy; ____ pills
CAMEO	2. Benson twins' jewelry
THOMAS	3. Second twin to die
TIMES	4. Had article about Harvey's mother; New York ___
BYARS	5. Author
CARLIE	6. Teenage girl sent to foster home
DYING	7. Carlie's Number One Rule as a nurse; No ___
CHER	8. Carlie's favorite stars; Sonny and _____
FOOTBALL	9. How Harvey explains his broken legs; ___ injury
FUNERALS	10. Where Thomas J went with Mr. Mason
PUPPY	11. Gift Thomas J and Carlie gave Harvey
HALTERS	12. Carlie learned to sew these
COINS	13. Gift from twins to Thomas J; gold ___
AUGUST	14. Month of birthday for Carlie and Thomas J
SNOOPY	15. Thomas wore a ___ t-shirt when dropped off
LETTER	16. What Carlie hoped would come from her mother
BARBER	17. Where Thomas J went for a real haircut
YOGA	18. Classes Harvey's mother took
ERASER	19. What Carlie wants to use on the bad memories
HARVEY	20. Boy with two legs in casts

Pinballs Fill In The Blank 4

_____ 1. Harvey made these and learned about himself

_____ 2. Where Thomas J went with Mr. Mason

_____ 3. Thomas J's favorite bible story; Baby ___

_____ 4. Had article about Harvey's mother; New York ___

_____ 5. Number of stepfathers Carlie has

_____ 6. Carlie couldn't be one due to bad grades

_____ 7. What Carlie hoped would come from her mother

_____ 8. Place Harvey's dad wanted to go

_____ 9. Harvey's birthday present

_____ 10. Boy with two legs in casts

_____ 11. Harvey's mother's new name at the commune

_____ 12. Carlie's famous dessert for Harvey; ___ cake

_____ 13. Where Carlie takes Harvey in his wheelchair

_____ 14. Gift Thomas J and Carlie gave Harvey

_____ 15. Benson twins don't believe in it

_____ 16. Carlie lost this & Thomas J found it

_____ 17. Picture in article shows Harvey's mom making one

_____ 18. Benson twins' jewelry

_____ 19. How Thomas J spoke

_____ 20. Author

Pinballs Fill In The Blank 4 Answer Key

LISTS	1. Harvey made these and learned about himself
FUNERALS	2. Where Thomas J went with Mr. Mason
MOSES	3. Thomas J's favorite bible story; Baby ___
TIMES	4. Had article about Harvey's mother; New York ___
TWO	5. Number of stepfathers Carlie has
MAJORETTE	6. Carlie couldn't be one due to bad grades
LETTER	7. What Carlie hoped would come from her mother
ELKS	8. Place Harvey's dad wanted to go
TV	9. Harvey's birthday present
HARVEY	10. Boy with two legs in casts
BETHENIA	11. Harvey's mother's new name at the commune
MAYONNAISE	12. Carlie's famous dessert for Harvey; ___ cake
LIBRARY	13. Where Carlie takes Harvey in his wheelchair
PUPPY	14. Gift Thomas J and Carlie gave Harvey
CANDY	15. Benson twins don't believe in it
EARRING	16. Carlie lost this & Thomas J found it
HAMMOCK	17. Picture in article shows Harvey's mom making one
CAMEO	18. Benson twins' jewelry
SHOUTED	19. How Thomas J spoke
BYARS	20. Author

Pinballs Matching 1

___ 1. PUPPY A. Mr. Mason told Thomas J about bumping Mr. Joe's ____
___ 2. MAJORETTE B. Number of stepfathers Carlie has
___ 3. CAMEO C. Silver cake decorations
___ 4. TIMES D. Carlie couldn't be one due to bad grades
___ 5. COINS E. Harvey's father drank these to forget
___ 6. MARTINIS F. Benson twins don't believe in it
___ 7. FOOTBALL G. Gift from twins to Thomas J; gold ___
___ 8. AUGUST H. Month of birthday for Carlie and Thomas J
___ 9. DECORETTES I. Carlie says they have no control over themselves
___ 10. TWO J. Benson twins' jewelry
___ 11. GRANDAM K. First twin to die; _____ Benson
___ 12. PINBALLS L. Had article about Harvey's mother; New York ___
___ 13. CASTS M. Vocation Carlie has chosen; Good Luck ____
___ 14. NURSE N. Carlie's favorite show; Young and The ___
___ 15. BETHENIA O. How Harvey explains his broken legs; ___ injury
___ 16. CARLIE P. Harvey has two of these
___ 17. XEROX Q. Book Benson twins gave Thomas J; Big ___ Stories
___ 18. RESTLESS R. Gift Thomas J and Carlie gave Harvey
___ 19. BIBLE S. Harvey made these and learned about himself
___ 20. SNOWBALL T. Teenage girl sent to foster home
___ 21. CASKET U. Harvey's guinea pig
___ 22. KFC V. Food to which Harvey was addicted
___ 23. LISTS W. Harvey's copy of his mother's article
___ 24. CANDY X. Harvey's dad's car
___ 25. JEFFERSON Y. Harvey's mother's new name at the commune

Pinballs Matching 1 Answer Key

R - 1. PUPPY	A.	Mr. Mason told Thomas J about bumping Mr. Joe's ____
D - 2. MAJORETTE	B.	Number of stepfathers Carlie has
J - 3. CAMEO	C.	Silver cake decorations
L - 4. TIMES	D.	Carlie couldn't be one due to bad grades
G - 5. COINS	E.	Harvey's father drank these to forget
E - 6. MARTINIS	F.	Benson twins don't believe in it
O - 7. FOOTBALL	G.	Gift from twins to Thomas J; gold ____
H - 8. AUGUST	H.	Month of birthday for Carlie and Thomas J
C - 9. DECORETTES	I.	Carlie says they have no control over themselves
B - 10. TWO	J.	Benson twins' jewelry
X - 11. GRANDAM	K.	First twin to die; _____ Benson
I - 12. PINBALLS	L.	Had article about Harvey's mother; New York ____
P - 13. CASTS	M.	Vocation Carlie has chosen; Good Luck ____
M - 14. NURSE	N.	Carlie's favorite show; Young and The ____
Y - 15. BETHENIA	O.	How Harvey explains his broken legs; ____ injury
T - 16. CARLIE	P.	Harvey has two of these
W - 17. XEROX	Q.	Book Benson twins gave Thomas J; Big ____ Stories
N - 18. RESTLESS	R.	Gift Thomas J and Carlie gave Harvey
Q - 19. BIBLE	S.	Harvey made these and learned about himself
U - 20. SNOWBALL	T.	Teenage girl sent to foster home
A - 21. CASKET	U.	Harvey's guinea pig
V - 22. KFC	V.	Food to which Harvey was addicted
S - 23. LISTS	W.	Harvey's copy of his mother's article
F - 24. CANDY	X.	Harvey's dad's car
K - 25. JEFFERSON	Y.	Harvey's mother's new name at the commune

Pinballs Matching 2

___ 1. MASON   A. Food to which Harvey was addicted
___ 2. BARBER   B. Thomas wore a ___ t-shirt when dropped off
___ 3. EARRING   C. Vocation Carlie has chosen; Good Luck ____
___ 4. BYARS   D. Where Thomas J went for a real haircut
___ 5. PINBALLS   E. What Carlie wants to use on the bad memories
___ 6. KFC   F. Harvey's father drank these to forget
___ 7. YOGA   G. Place Harvey's dad wanted to go
___ 8. MOSES   H. Author
___ 9. LIBRARY   I. Funny present for Harvey's puppy; ____ pills
___10. CASTS   J. Thomas J's favorite bible story; Baby ___
___11. ERASER   K. Carlie, Thomas J, & Harvey's foster mother; Mrs. ___
___12. CARLIE   L. Harvey's dad's car
___13. MAJORETTE   M. Harvey's copy of his mother's article
___14. WORM   N. First twin to die; _____ Benson
___15. GRANDAM   O. Where Carlie takes Harvey in his wheelchair
___16. DAWN   P. Benson twins' favorite TV show; Tony Orlando & ___
___17. NURSE   Q. Carlie couldn't be one due to bad grades
___18. TWO   R. Carlie lost this & Thomas J found it
___19. MARTINIS   S. Teenage girl sent to foster home
___20. RESTLESS   T. Classes Harvey's mother took
___21. SNOOPY   U. Harvey has two of these
___22. COINS   V. Carlie's favorite show; Young and The ___
___23. ELKS   W. Number of stepfathers Carlie has
___24. XEROX   X. Gift from twins to Thomas J; gold ___
___25. JEFFERSON   Y. Carlie says they have no control over themselves

Copyrighted

Pinballs Matching 2 Answer Key

K - 1. MASON	A.	Food to which Harvey was addicted
D - 2. BARBER	B.	Thomas wore a ___ t-shirt when dropped off
R - 3. EARRING	C.	Vocation Carlie has chosen; Good Luck ___
H - 4. BYARS	D.	Where Thomas J went for a real haircut
Y - 5. PINBALLS	E.	What Carlie wants to use on the bad memories
A - 6. KFC	F.	Harvey's father drank these to forget
T - 7. YOGA	G.	Place Harvey's dad wanted to go
J - 8. MOSES	H.	Author
O - 9. LIBRARY	I.	Funny present for Harvey's puppy; ___ pills
U -10. CASTS	J.	Thomas J's favorite bible story; Baby ___
E -11. ERASER	K.	Carlie, Thomas J, & Harvey's foster mother; Mrs. ___
S -12. CARLIE	L.	Harvey's dad's car
Q -13. MAJORETTE	M.	Harvey's copy of his mother's article
I - 14. WORM	N.	First twin to die; ___ Benson
L - 15. GRANDAM	O.	Where Carlie takes Harvey in his wheelchair
P - 16. DAWN	P.	Benson twins' favorite TV show; Tony Orlando & ___
C - 17. NURSE	Q.	Carlie couldn't be one due to bad grades
W -18. TWO	R.	Carlie lost this & Thomas J found it
F - 19. MARTINIS	S.	Teenage girl sent to foster home
V -20. RESTLESS	T.	Classes Harvey's mother took
B -21. SNOOPY	U.	Harvey has two of these
X -22. COINS	V.	Carlie's favorite show; Young and The ___
G -23. ELKS	W.	Number of stepfathers Carlie has
M -24. XEROX	X.	Gift from twins to Thomas J; gold ___
N -25. JEFFERSON	Y.	Carlie says they have no control over themselves

Pinballs Matching 3

___ 1. JEFFERSON   A. Classes Harvey's mother took
___ 2. THOMAS   B. Boy with two legs in casts
___ 3. YOGA   C. Book Benson twins gave Thomas J; Big ___ Stories
___ 4. PINBALL   D. Place Harvey's dad wanted to go
___ 5. HALTERS   E. Benson twins don't believe in it
___ 6. CANDY   F. Author
___ 7. LIBRARY   G. Carlie learned to sew these
___ 8. CAMEO   H. Where Carlie takes Harvey in his wheelchair
___ 9. ELKS   I. Benson twins' favorite TV show; Tony Orlando & ___
___10. CONSTRUCTION   J. Second twin to die
___11. ERASER   K. Carlie says they have no control over themselves
___12. NURSE   L. Thomas J's favorite bible story; Baby ___
___13. LETTER   M. Gift Thomas J and Carlie gave Harvey
___14. CASKET   N. Vocation Carlie has chosen; Good Luck ___
___15. DECORETTES   O. Harvey has two of these
___16. BIBLE   P. Harvey's mother's new name at the commune
___17. DAWN   Q. Carlie compares one to her life; ___ machine
___18. HARVEY   R. What Carlie hoped would come from her mother
___19. MOSES   S. Benson twins' jewelry
___20. PINBALLS   T. What Carlie wants to use on the bad memories
___21. WORM   U. Funny present for Harvey's puppy; ___ pills
___22. PUPPY   V. Silver cake decorations
___23. BETHENIA   W. Mr. Mason told Thomas J about bumping Mr. Joe's ___
___24. BYARS   X. First twin to die; ___ Benson
___25. CASTS   Y. Business of Harvey's dad

Pinballs Matching 3 Answer Key

X - 1. JEFFERSON	A.	Classes Harvey's mother took
J - 2. THOMAS	B.	Boy with two legs in casts
A - 3. YOGA	C.	Book Benson twins gave Thomas J; Big ___ Stories
Q - 4. PINBALL	D.	Place Harvey's dad wanted to go
G - 5. HALTERS	E.	Benson twins don't believe in it
E - 6. CANDY	F.	Author
H - 7. LIBRARY	G.	Carlie learned to sew these
S - 8. CAMEO	H.	Where Carlie takes Harvey in his wheelchair
D - 9. ELKS	I.	Benson twins' favorite TV show; Tony Orlando & ___
Y - 10. CONSTRUCTION	J.	Second twin to die
T - 11. ERASER	K.	Carlie says they have no control over themselves
N - 12. NURSE	L.	Thomas J's favorite bible story; Baby ___
R - 13. LETTER	M.	Gift Thomas J and Carlie gave Harvey
W - 14. CASKET	N.	Vocation Carlie has chosen; Good Luck ___
V - 15. DECORETTES	O.	Harvey has two of these
C - 16. BIBLE	P.	Harvey's mother's new name at the commune
I - 17. DAWN	Q.	Carlie compares one to her life; ___ machine
B - 18. HARVEY	R.	What Carlie hoped would come from her mother
L - 19. MOSES	S.	Benson twins' jewelry
K - 20. PINBALLS	T.	What Carlie wants to use on the bad memories
U - 21. WORM	U.	Funny present for Harvey's puppy; ___ pills
M - 22. PUPPY	V.	Silver cake decorations
P - 23. BETHENIA	W.	Mr. Mason told Thomas J about bumping Mr. Joe's ___
F - 24. BYARS	X.	First twin to die; ___ Benson
O - 25. CASTS	Y.	Business of Harvey's dad

Pinballs Matching 4

___ 1. NURSE   A. Picture in article shows Harvey's mom making one
___ 2. CHER   B. Harvey's guinea pig
___ 3. PINBALL   C. Carlie lost this & Thomas J found it
___ 4. BETHENIA   D. Carlie's Number One Rule as a nurse; No ___
___ 5. PINBALLS   E. Number of stepfathers Carlie has
___ 6. LISTS   F. Harvey's birthday present
___ 7. CAMEO   G. Carlie says they have no control over themselves
___ 8. DYING   H. Thomas wore a ___ t-shirt when dropped off
___ 9. SNOWBALL   I. Harvey made these and learned about himself
___ 10. HARVEY   J. Boy with two legs in casts
___ 11. DECORETTES   K. Harvey's father drank these to forget
___ 12. VIRGINIA   L. Harvey's mother's new name at the commune
___ 13. FOOTBALL   M. How Harvey explains his broken legs; ___ injury
___ 14. THOMAS   N. Harvey's dad's car
___ 15. MARTINIS   O. Where Harvey's mother makes hammocks
___ 16. COINS   P. Carlie wanted to put them on Harvey's toes
___ 17. SNOOPY   Q. Carlie's favorite stars; Sonny and _____
___ 18. CASTS   R. Mr. Mason told Thomas J about bumping Mr. Joe's ___
___ 19. HAMMOCK   S. Second twin to die
___ 20. TV   T. Gift from twins to Thomas J; gold ___
___ 21. CASKET   U. Vocation Carlie has chosen; Good Luck ___
___ 22. DECALS   V. Carlie compares one to her life; ___ machine
___ 23. EARRING   W. Silver cake decorations
___ 24. GRANDAM   X. Benson twins' jewelry
___ 25. TWO   Y. Harvey has two of these

Pinballs Matching 4 Answer Key

U - 1. NURSE		A. Picture in article shows Harvey's mom making one
Q - 2. CHER		B. Harvey's guinea pig
V - 3. PINBALL		C. Carlie lost this & Thomas J found it
L - 4. BETHENIA		D. Carlie's Number One Rule as a nurse; No ___
G - 5. PINBALLS		E. Number of stepfathers Carlie has
I - 6. LISTS		F. Harvey's birthday present
X - 7. CAMEO		G. Carlie says they have no control over themselves
D - 8. DYING		H. Thomas wore a ___ t-shirt when dropped off
B - 9. SNOWBALL		I. Harvey made these and learned about himself
J - 10. HARVEY		J. Boy with two legs in casts
W - 11. DECORETTES		K. Harvey's father drank these to forget
O - 12. VIRGINIA		L. Harvey's mother's new name at the commune
M - 13. FOOTBALL		M. How Harvey explains his broken legs; ___ injury
S - 14. THOMAS		N. Harvey's dad's car
K - 15. MARTINIS		O. Where Harvey's mother makes hammocks
T - 16. COINS		P. Carlie wanted to put them on Harvey's toes
H - 17. SNOOPY		Q. Carlie's favorite stars; Sonny and _____
Y - 18. CASTS		R. Mr. Mason told Thomas J about bumping Mr. Joe's ____
A - 19. HAMMOCK		S. Second twin to die
F - 20. TV		T. Gift from twins to Thomas J; gold ___
R - 21. CASKET		U. Vocation Carlie has chosen; Good Luck ____
P - 22. DECALS		V. Carlie compares one to her life; ___ machine
C - 23. EARRING		W. Silver cake decorations
N - 24. GRANDAM		X. Benson twins' jewelry
E - 25. TWO		Y. Harvey has two of these

Pinballs Magic Squares 1

Match the definition with the vocabulary word. Put your answers in the magic squares below. When your answers are correct, all columns and rows will add to the same number.

A. MAYONNAISE
B. FUNERALS
C. BETHENIA
D. DAWN
E. CHER
F. CANDY
G. VIRGINIA
H. MARTINIS
I. CASTS
J. PINBALL
K. BARBER
L. CARLIE
M. KFC
N. HALTERS
O. ELKS
P. SNOOPY

1. Harvey's father drank these to forget
2. Carlie's famous dessert for Harvey; ___ cake
3. Where Thomas J went with Mr. Mason
4. Where Harvey's mother makes hammocks
5. Carlie compares one to her life; ___ machine
6. Place Harvey's dad wanted to go
7. Thomas wore a ___ t-shirt when dropped off
8. Harvey has two of these
9. Where Thomas J went for a real haircut
10. Carlie learned to sew these
11. Food to which Harvey was addicted
12. Teenage girl sent to foster home
13. Carlie's favorite stars; Sonny and _____
14. Benson twins' favorite TV show; Tony Orlando & ___
15. Harvey's mother's new name at the commune
16. Benson twins don't believe in it

A=	B=	C=	D=
E=	F=	G=	H=
I=	J=	K=	L=
M=	N=	O=	P=

Pinballs Magic Squares 1 Answer Key

Match the definition with the vocabulary word. Put your answers in the magic squares below. When your answers are correct, all columns and rows will add to the same number.

A. MAYONNAISE
B. FUNERALS
C. BETHENIA
D. DAWN
E. CHER
F. CANDY
G. VIRGINIA
H. MARTINIS
I. CASTS
J. PINBALL
K. BARBER
L. CARLIE
M. KFC
N. HALTERS
O. ELKS
P. SNOOPY

1. Harvey's father drank these to forget
2. Carlie's famous dessert for Harvey; ___ cake
3. Where Thomas J went with Mr. Mason
4. Where Harvey's mother makes hammocks
5. Carlie compares one to her life; ___ machine
6. Place Harvey's dad wanted to go
7. Thomas wore a ___ t-shirt when dropped off
8. Harvey has two of these
9. Where Thomas J went for a real haircut
10. Carlie learned to sew these
11. Food to which Harvey was addicted
12. Teenage girl sent to foster home
13. Carlie's favorite stars; Sonny and _____
14. Benson twins' favorite TV show; Tony Orlando & ___
15. Harvey's mother's new name at the commune
16. Benson twins don't believe in it

A=2	B=3	C=15	D=14
E=13	F=16	G=4	H=1
I=8	J=5	K=9	L=12
M=11	N=10	O=6	P=7

Pinballs Magic Squares 2

Match the definition with the vocabulary word. Put your answers in the magic squares below. When your answers are correct, all columns and rows will add to the same number.

A. PINBALL
B. XEROX
C. FOOTBALL
D. CANDY
E. TIMES
F. DAWN
G. HAMMOCK
H. MOSES
I. EARRING
J. HALTERS
K. MASON
L. CAMEO
M. MAJORETTE
N. GRANDAM
O. CASKET
P. COINS

1. Mr. Mason told Thomas J about bumping Mr. Joe's ____
2. Carlie learned to sew these
3. Thomas J's favorite bible story; Baby ____
4. Carlie compares one to her life; ____ machine
5. Benson twins don't believe in it
6. Had article about Harvey's mother; New York ____
7. Carlie, Thomas J, & Harvey's foster mother; Mrs. ____
8. Harvey's dad's car
9. Benson twins' favorite TV show; Tony Orlando & ____
10. How Harvey explains his broken legs; ____ injury
11. Carlie couldn't be one due to bad grades
12. Benson twins' jewelry
13. Carlie lost this & Thomas J found it
14. Gift from twins to Thomas J; gold ____
15. Harvey's copy of his mother's article
16. Picture in article shows Harvey's mom making one

A=	B=	C=	D=
E=	F=	G=	H=
I=	J=	K=	L=
M=	N=	O=	P=

Pinballs Magic Squares 2 Answer Key

Match the definition with the vocabulary word. Put your answers in the magic squares below. When your answers are correct, all columns and rows will add to the same number.

A. PINBALL
B. XEROX
C. FOOTBALL
D. CANDY
E. TIMES
F. DAWN
G. HAMMOCK
H. MOSES
I. EARRING
J. HALTERS
K. MASON
L. CAMEO
M. MAJORETTE
N. GRANDAM
O. CASKET
P. COINS

1. Mr. Mason told Thomas J about bumping Mr. Joe's ____
2. Carlie learned to sew these
3. Thomas J's favorite bible story; Baby ____
4. Carlie compares one to her life; ____ machine
5. Benson twins don't believe in it
6. Had article about Harvey's mother; New York ____
7. Carlie, Thomas J, & Harvey's foster mother; Mrs. ____
8. Harvey's dad's car
9. Benson twins' favorite TV show; Tony Orlando & ____
10. How Harvey explains his broken legs; ____ injury
11. Carlie couldn't be one due to bad grades
12. Benson twins' jewelry
13. Carlie lost this & Thomas J found it
14. Gift from twins to Thomas J; gold ____
15. Harvey's copy of his mother's article
16. Picture in article shows Harvey's mom making one

A=4	B=15	C=10	D=5
E=6	F=9	G=16	H=3
I=13	J=2	K=7	L=12
M=11	N=8	O=1	P=14

Pinballs Magic Squares 3

Match the definition with the vocabulary word. Put your answers in the magic squares below. When your answers are correct, all columns and rows will add to the same number.

A. CHER
B. RESTLESS
C. THOMAS
D. PINBALL
E. CASTS
F. ERASER
G. TWO
H. CONSTRUCTION
I. TIMES
J. KFC
K. FOOTBALL
L. COINS
M. MOSES
N. WORM
O. JEFFERSON
P. CANDY

1. Second twin to die
2. Food to which Harvey was addicted
3. What Carlie wants to use on the bad memories
4. First twin to die; _____ Benson
5. Benson twins don't believe in it
6. Harvey has two of these
7. Had article about Harvey's mother; New York ___
8. Carlie compares one to her life; ___ machine
9. Thomas J's favorite bible story; Baby ___
10. Business of Harvey's dad
11. Gift from twins to Thomas J; gold ___
12. Carlie's favorite stars; Sonny and _____
13. Carlie's favorite show; Young and The ___
14. How Harvey explains his broken legs; ___ injury
15. Number of stepfathers Carlie has
16. Funny present for Harvey's puppy; ____ pills

A=	B=	C=	D=
E=	F=	G=	H=
I=	J=	K=	L=
M=	N=	O=	P=

Pinballs Magic Squares 3 Answer Key

Match the definition with the vocabulary word. Put your answers in the magic squares below. When your answers are correct, all columns and rows will add to the same number.

A. CHER
B. RESTLESS
C. THOMAS
D. PINBALL
E. CASTS
F. ERASER
G. TWO
H. CONSTRUCTION
I. TIMES
J. KFC
K. FOOTBALL
L. COINS
M. MOSES
N. WORM
O. JEFFERSON
P. CANDY

1. Second twin to die
2. Food to which Harvey was addicted
3. What Carlie wants to use on the bad memories
4. First twin to die; _____ Benson
5. Benson twins don't believe in it
6. Harvey has two of these
7. Had article about Harvey's mother; New York ___
8. Carlie compares one to her life; ___ machine
9. Thomas J's favorite bible story; Baby ___
10. Business of Harvey's dad
11. Gift from twins to Thomas J; gold ___
12. Carlie's favorite stars; Sonny and _____
13. Carlie's favorite show; Young and The ___
14. How Harvey explains his broken legs; ___ injury
15. Number of stepfathers Carlie has
16. Funny present for Harvey's puppy; _____ pills

A=12	B=13	C=1	D=8
E=6	F=3	G=15	H=10
I=7	J=2	K=14	L=11
M=9	N=16	O=4	P=5

Pinballs Magic Squares 4

Match the definition with the vocabulary word. Put your answers in the magic squares below. When your answers are correct, all columns and rows will add to the same number.

A. LIBRARY
B. HARVEY
C. LISTS
D. ERASER
E. CAMEO
F. COINS
G. BYARS
H. DECALS
I. MAYONNAISE
J. TIMES
K. CHER
L. DECORETTES
M. GRANDAM
N. MOSES
O. TV
P. EARRING

1. Gift from twins to Thomas J; gold ___
2. Carlie's famous dessert for Harvey; ___ cake
3. Harvey's birthday present
4. What Carlie wants to use on the bad memories
5. Harvey's dad's car
6. Boy with two legs in casts
7. Carlie wanted to put them on Harvey's toes
8. Carlie's favorite stars; Sonny and _____
9. Harvey made these and learned about himself
10. Carlie lost this & Thomas J found it
11. Had article about Harvey's mother; New York ___
12. Benson twins' jewelry
13. Silver cake decorations
14. Author
15. Where Carlie takes Harvey in his wheelchair
16. Thomas J's favorite bible story; Baby ___

A=	B=	C=	D=
E=	F=	G=	H=
I=	J=	K=	L=
M=	N=	O=	P=

Pinballs Magic Squares 4 Answer Key

Match the definition with the vocabulary word. Put your answers in the magic squares below. When your answers are correct, all columns and rows will add to the same number.

A. LIBRARY
B. HARVEY
C. LISTS
D. ERASER
E. CAMEO
F. COINS
G. BYARS
H. DECALS
I. MAYONNAISE
J. TIMES
K. CHER
L. DECORETTES
M. GRANDAM
N. MOSES
O. TV
P. EARRING

1. Gift from twins to Thomas J; gold ___
2. Carlie's famous dessert for Harvey; ___ cake
3. Harvey's birthday present
4. What Carlie wants to use on the bad memories
5. Harvey's dad's car
6. Boy with two legs in casts
7. Carlie wanted to put them on Harvey's toes
8. Carlie's favorite stars; Sonny and _____
9. Harvey made these and learned about himself
10. Carlie lost this & Thomas J found it
11. Had article about Harvey's mother; New York ___
12. Benson twins' jewelry
13. Silver cake decorations
14. Author
15. Where Carlie takes Harvey in his wheelchair
16. Thomas J's favorite bible story; Baby ___

A=15	B=6	C=9	D=4
E=12	F=1	G=14	H=7
I=2	J=11	K=8	L=13
M=5	N=16	O=3	P=10

Pinballs Word Search 1

```
S P K D C W J D Y R T S U G U A W B
N U M N O X P E O E K B N C A N D Y
O P G A N E G C G S K I P L K Y O R
W P L I S T S A A A R L I D A W N Y
B Y Q R T O C L R R Q B N Q T M Q H
A X U C R X N S A E R C B E R E H C
L N R M U Y D E S A B R A B L B F H
L S R L C E B A R B E R L M Q K W J
H O F D T V F Y A Q X E L N E Y S X
W V O U I R W K Y R T H S N O O P Y
T X O M O A L C B T M A R T I N I S
J H T O N H A K E Y D M C A S K E T
S N B S F S L R L J R M L P G Z S P
H K A E T H O M A S X O R E X N C G
M D L S J K E I L R A C T G I Y Q Q
D H L G R A N D A M S K K O C L G Q
H A L T E R S E M I T J C B I B L E
```

Author (5)
Benson twins don't believe in it (5)
Benson twins' favorite TV show; Tony Orlando & ___ (4)
Benson twins' jewelry (5)
Book Benson twins gave Thomas J; Big ___ Stories (5)
Boy with two legs in casts (6)
Business of Harvey's dad (12)
Carlie learned to sew these (7)
Carlie lost this & Thomas J found it (7)
Carlie says they have no control over themselves (8)
Carlie wanted to put them on Harvey's toes (6)
Carlie's favorite stars; Sonny and _____ (4)
Carlie, Thomas J, & Harvey's foster mother; Mrs. ___ (5)
Classes Harvey's mother took (4)
Food to which Harvey was addicted (3)
Funny present for Harvey's puppy; ____ pills (4)
Gift Thomas J and Carlie gave Harvey (5)
Gift from twins to Thomas J; gold ___ (5)
Had article about Harvey's mother; New York ___ (5)
Harvey has two of these (5)
Harvey made these and learned about himself (5)

Harvey's birthday present (2)
Harvey's copy of his mother's article (5)
Harvey's dad's car (7)
Harvey's father drank these to forget (8)
Harvey's guinea pig (8)
How Harvey explains his broken legs; ___ injury (8)
How Thomas J spoke (7)
Month of birthday for Carlie and Thomas J (6)
Mr. Mason told Thomas J about bumping Mr. Joe's ____ (6)
Number of stepfathers Carlie has (3)
Picture in article shows Harvey's mom making one (7)
Place Harvey's dad wanted to go (4)
Second twin to die (6)
Teenage girl sent to foster home (6)
Thomas J's favorite bible story; Baby ___ (5)
Thomas wore a ___ t-shirt when dropped off (6)
Vocation Carlie has chosen; Good Luck ____ (5)
What Carlie hoped would come from her mother (6)
What Carlie wants to use on the bad memories (6)
Where Carlie takes Harvey in his wheelchair (7)
Where Thomas J went for a real haircut (6)

Pinballs Word Search 1 Answer Key

Author (5)
Benson twins don't believe in it (5)
Benson twins' favorite TV show; Tony Orlando & ___ (4)
Benson twins' jewelry (5)
Book Benson twins gave Thomas J; Big ___ Stories (5)
Boy with two legs in casts (6)
Business of Harvey's dad (12)
Carlie learned to sew these (7)
Carlie lost this & Thomas J found it (7)
Carlie says they have no control over themselves (8)
Carlie wanted to put them on Harvey's toes (6)
Carlie's favorite stars; Sonny and _____ (4)
Carlie, Thomas J, & Harvey's foster mother; Mrs. ___ (5)
Classes Harvey's mother took (4)
Food to which Harvey was addicted (3)
Funny present for Harvey's puppy; ____ pills (4)
Gift Thomas J and Carlie gave Harvey (5)
Gift from twins to Thomas J; gold ___ (5)
Had article about Harvey's mother; New York ___ (5)
Harvey has two of these (5)
Harvey made these and learned about himself (5)

Harvey's birthday present (2)
Harvey's copy of his mother's article (5)
Harvey's dad's car (7)
Harvey's father drank these to forget (8)
Harvey's guinea pig (8)
How Harvey explains his broken legs; ___ injury (8)
How Thomas J spoke (7)
Month of birthday for Carlie and Thomas J (6)
Mr. Mason told Thomas J about bumping Mr. Joe's ____ (6)
Number of stepfathers Carlie has (3)
Picture in article shows Harvey's mom making one (7)
Place Harvey's dad wanted to go (4)
Second twin to die (6)
Teenage girl sent to foster home (6)
Thomas J's favorite bible story; Baby ___ (5)
Thomas wore a ___ t-shirt when dropped off (6)
Vocation Carlie has chosen; Good Luck ____ (5)
What Carlie hoped would come from her mother (6)
What Carlie wants to use on the bad memories (6)
Where Carlie takes Harvey in his wheelchair (7)
Where Thomas J went for a real haircut (6)

Pinballs Word Search 2

```
H S N O O P Y F O O T B A L L T R K
A N T B Y G R W B A R B E R E S K K
M O E S I A N N O Y A M R K B H X Z
M W D D Q N U S B R N T S A M O H T
O B E K Y H S G B J M A T J W U X M
C A C J D E A G U Y C Q I X S T Y W
K L A P L W K L S S A P M C N E E Z
P L L T M W F D T D T R E O C D V B
L U S N I O C H C E L K S C H E R C
H E P M B A S A B O R A P Q W E A R
R L R P R E M E S W M S D G T M H K
B Y V L Y A L I S T S E R T E X C R
I T I W D R H S D J S X E O Z E A G
B E S N Q R S Y V R L S X B R N P
L D A W N I I Y U Y O G A M X O D K
E R V T R N W N Y V H L R C W X Y Z
G D J Y G G T L J E F F E R S O N
```

Author (5)
Benson twins don't believe in it (5)
Benson twins' favorite TV show; Tony Orlando & ___ (4)
Benson twins' jewelry (5)
Book Benson twins gave Thomas J; Big ___ Stories (5)
Boy with two legs in casts (6)
Carlie learned to sew these (7)
Carlie lost this & Thomas J found it (7)
Carlie wanted to put them on Harvey's toes (6)
Carlie's Number One Rule as a nurse; No ___ (5)
Carlie's famous dessert for Harvey; ___ cake (10)
Carlie's favorite show; Young and The ___ (8)
Carlie's favorite stars; Sonny and _____ (4)
Carlie, Thomas J, & Harvey's foster mother; Mrs. ___ (5)
Classes Harvey's mother took (4)
First twin to die; _____ Benson (9)
Food to which Harvey was addicted (3)
Funny present for Harvey's puppy; ____ pills (4)
Gift Thomas J and Carlie gave Harvey (5)
Gift from twins to Thomas J; gold ___ (5)
Had article about Harvey's mother; New York ___ (5)
Harvey has two of these (5)
Harvey made these and learned about himself (5)
Harvey's birthday present (2)
Harvey's copy of his mother's article (5)
Harvey's dad's car (7)
Harvey's guinea pig (8)
How Harvey explains his broken legs; ___ injury (8)
How Thomas J spoke (7)
Month of birthday for Carlie and Thomas J (6)
Mr. Mason told Thomas J about bumping Mr. Joe's ____ (6)
Number of stepfathers Carlie has (3)
Picture in article shows Harvey's mom making one (7)
Place Harvey's dad wanted to go (4)
Second twin to die (6)
Teenage girl sent to foster home (6)
Thomas J's favorite bible story; Baby ___ (5)
Thomas wore a ___ t-shirt when dropped off (6)
Vocation Carlie has chosen; Good Luck ____ (5)
What Carlie hoped would come from her mother (6)
What Carlie wants to use on the bad memories (6)
Where Thomas J went for a real haircut (6)

Pinballs Word Search 2 Answer Key

```
H  S  N  O  O  P  Y  F  O  O  T  B  A  L  L  T
A  N              W  B  A  R  B  E  R  E     S
M  O  E  S  I  A  N  N  O  Y  A  M     K     H
M  W  D           U  S     R        S  A  M  O  H  T
O  B  E        H  S  G  B     M  A     T     U
C  A  C        E  A     U  Y  C        I     T     Y
K  L  A     L     K  L     S  A     M  N     E     E
P  L  L  T  M     F     T     T  R  E  O     D  V
   U  S  N  I  O  C        E  L  K  S  C  H  E  R  C
      E  P     A  S  A     O  R  A           E     A
R        P  R  E  M  E  S  W  M  S        T  M     H
B     V  L  Y  A  L  I  S  T  S  E  R  T  E  X     C
I  T     I     D  R     D     S     E  O     E  A
B  E     N  R        Y     R     L  S        R  N
L  D  A  W  N  I     I  U  Y  O  G  A        O  D
E  R              N        N           R     X  Y
G              G  G        J  E  F  F  E  R  S  O  N
```

Author (5)
Benson twins don't believe in it (5)
Benson twins' favorite TV show; Tony Orlando & ___ (4)
Benson twins' jewelry (5)
Book Benson twins gave Thomas J; Big ___ Stories (5)
Boy with two legs in casts (6)
Carlie learned to sew these (7)
Carlie lost this & Thomas J found it (7)
Carlie wanted to put them on Harvey's toes (6)
Carlie's Number One Rule as a nurse; No ___ (5)
Carlie's famous dessert for Harvey; ___ cake (10)
Carlie's favorite show; Young and The ___ (8)
Carlie's favorite stars; Sonny and _____ (4)
Carlie, Thomas J, & Harvey's foster mother; Mrs. ___ (5)
Classes Harvey's mother took (4)
First twin to die; _____ Benson (9)
Food to which Harvey was addicted (3)
Funny present for Harvey's puppy; ____ pills (4)
Gift Thomas J and Carlie gave Harvey (5)
Gift from twins to Thomas J; gold ___ (5)
Had article about Harvey's mother; New York ___ (5)

Harvey has two of these (5)
Harvey made these and learned about himself (5)
Harvey's birthday present (2)
Harvey's copy of his mother's article (5)
Harvey's dad's car (7)
Harvey's guinea pig (8)
How Harvey explains his broken legs; ___ injury (8)
How Thomas J spoke (7)
Month of birthday for Carlie and Thomas J (6)
Mr. Mason told Thomas J about bumping Mr. Joe's _____ (6)
Number of stepfathers Carlie has (3)
Picture in article shows Harvey's mom making one (7)
Place Harvey's dad wanted to go (4)
Second twin to die (6)
Teenage girl sent to foster home (6)
Thomas J's favorite bible story; Baby ___ (5)
Thomas wore a ___ t-shirt when dropped off (6)
Vocation Carlie has chosen; Good Luck ____ (5)
What Carlie hoped would come from her mother (6)
What Carlie wants to use on the bad memories (6)
Where Thomas J went for a real haircut (6)

Pinballs Word Search 3

```
Q G G F C H R P S X G J E C M B J Q B F
N T W R Y A W D L W F T R C P O W V Y D
M R W S S R S P A F F T A C A B S P A V
A F T Q R V S K C R N Q S G K M G E R V
U S X H S E T T E R O C E D F M E W S L
G Y K K M Y S T D T F A R S R A L O L L
U Q R I K R T T N K T R S O R Y B X J V
S T T J Z E K Z L H B L W P A O I T S Z
T W O T L C H E R E Z I Y W I N B W V S
C H H X I M N R K F S E O C N N U T P P
Z R O Z B L B C S M K S G W E A B R L L
K M D M R Z F S T P B M A G H I E A S T
B S T S A C S N O W B A L L T S S L L E
C N K L R S W O L L Q S R W E E P I K L
N I F A Y A Q O X L Z O P B B S Y S L S
G O Z R D F W P F C L N Y I E D D T B Z
M C X E R O X Y P P U P N F N R Y S K Z
A P H N G O P P S J Q S W A X B W N F F
R W A U R T D Q H Y H F C Z Z J A N Z P
T Q M F A B P D O H A L T E R S R L K D
I P M Z N A F T U H T R Q Z D Z Q B L G
N H O D D L Y R T V I R G I N I A C N S
I G C R A L X R E T T E R O J A M I W L
S Z K Y M L L Q D E A R R I N G Y J T C
J E F F E R S O N V P B X C N D S Q B V
```

AUGUST COINS HALTERS MAYONNAISE TIMES
BARBER DAWN HAMMOCK MOSES TV
BETHENIA DECALS HARVEY NURSE TWO
BIBLE DECORETTES JEFFERSON PINBALL VIRGINIA
BYARS DYING KFC PINBALLS WORM
CAMEO EARRING LETTER PUPPY XEROX
CANDY ELKS LIBRARY RESTLESS YOGA
CARLIE ERASER LISTS SHOUTED
CASKET FOOTBALL MAJORETTE SNOOPY
CASTS FUNERALS MARTINIS SNOWBALL
CHER GRANDAM MASON THOMAS

Pinballs Word Search 3 Answer Key

AUGUST	COINS	HALTERS	MAYONNAISE	TIMES
BARBER	DAWN	HAMMOCK	MOSES	TV
BETHENIA	DECALS	HARVEY	NURSE	TWO
BIBLE	DECORETTES	JEFFERSON	PINBALL	VIRGINIA
BYARS	DYING	KFC	PINBALLS	WORM
CAMEO	EARRING	LETTER	PUPPY	XEROX
CANDY	ELKS	LIBRARY	RESTLESS	YOGA
CARLIE	ERASER	LISTS	SHOUTED	
CASKET	FOOTBALL	MAJORETTE	SNOOPY	
CASTS	FUNERALS	MARTINIS	SNOWBALL	
CHER	GRANDAM	MASON	THOMAS	

Pinballs Word Search 4

```
M A D N A R G W A C M S L V F T P D J R
A T K C S C W B U J A N L I U I G E E G
Y B F N R G J Y G P R O G R N M F C F F
O L L A B N I P U K T W Y G E E S O F N
N B I W F S W P S G I B C I R S M R E C
N V W B T H P H T M N A O N A L R E R L
A T W S R Y M P W Q I L N I L L X T S C
I Z I K W A T D L H S L S A S A D T O Y
S L K L G B R V V L B G T V X B N E N T
E G L F G Z T Y S Q S H R Z H N S S X H
L V M H D Z C W T Z R N U E V I B H V R
W T O Y C O F D S T E C T S P Q O N Y R
J J S N I W T R M H T J T G K T N U Y Y
R W E N D V B W R F L H I C Z P L T D F
S T S A C A M E O M A J O R E T T E L M
X Y L A D N G O W I H M N M V D C D S B
G W N G X N T H N T M C E T A A T X M S
P D V O I B V E S A B A R A L S W D G R
Y W D Y A D H C H E I S L S R E S A R E
P P D L L T C A S F B K B R M R C W N S
O Z L Y E T F R R X L E N A N A I H X R
O D T B L Q U L L V E T Q Y R C S N E J
N H C Q K N M I K R E R H B F B W O G R
S C W B S H J E F X H Y O K H A E W N W
N Q D T J G Q N B M N R M X D X W R C Y
```

AUGUST	DAWN	JEFFERSON	PUPPY
BARBER	DECALS	KFC	RESTLESS
BETHENIA	DECORETTES	LETTER	SHOUTED
BIBLE	DYING	LIBRARY	SNOOPY
BYARS	EARRING	LISTS	SNOWBALL
CAMEO	ELKS	MAJORETTE	THOMAS
CANDY	ERASER	MARTINIS	TIMES
CARLIE	FOOTBALL	MASON	TV
CASKET	FUNERALS	MAYONNAISE	TWO
CASTS	GRANDAM	MOSES	VIRGINIA
CHER	HALTERS	NURSE	WORM
COINS	HAMMOCK	PINBALL	XEROX
CONSTRUCTION	HARVEY	PINBALLS	YOGA

Pinballs Word Search 4 Answer Key

AUGUST	DAWN	JEFFERSON	PUPPY
BARBER	DECALS	KFC	RESTLESS
BETHENIA	DECORETTES	LETTER	SHOUTED
BIBLE	DYING	LIBRARY	SNOOPY
BYARS	EARRING	LISTS	SNOWBALL
CAMEO	ELKS	MAJORETTE	THOMAS
CANDY	ERASER	MARTINIS	TIMES
CARLIE	FOOTBALL	MASON	TV
CASKET	FUNERALS	MAYONNAISE	TWO
CASTS	GRANDAM	MOSES	VIRGINIA
CHER	HALTERS	NURSE	WORM
COINS	HAMMOCK	PINBALL	XEROX
CONSTRUCTION	HARVEY	PINBALLS	YOGA

Pinballs Crossword 1

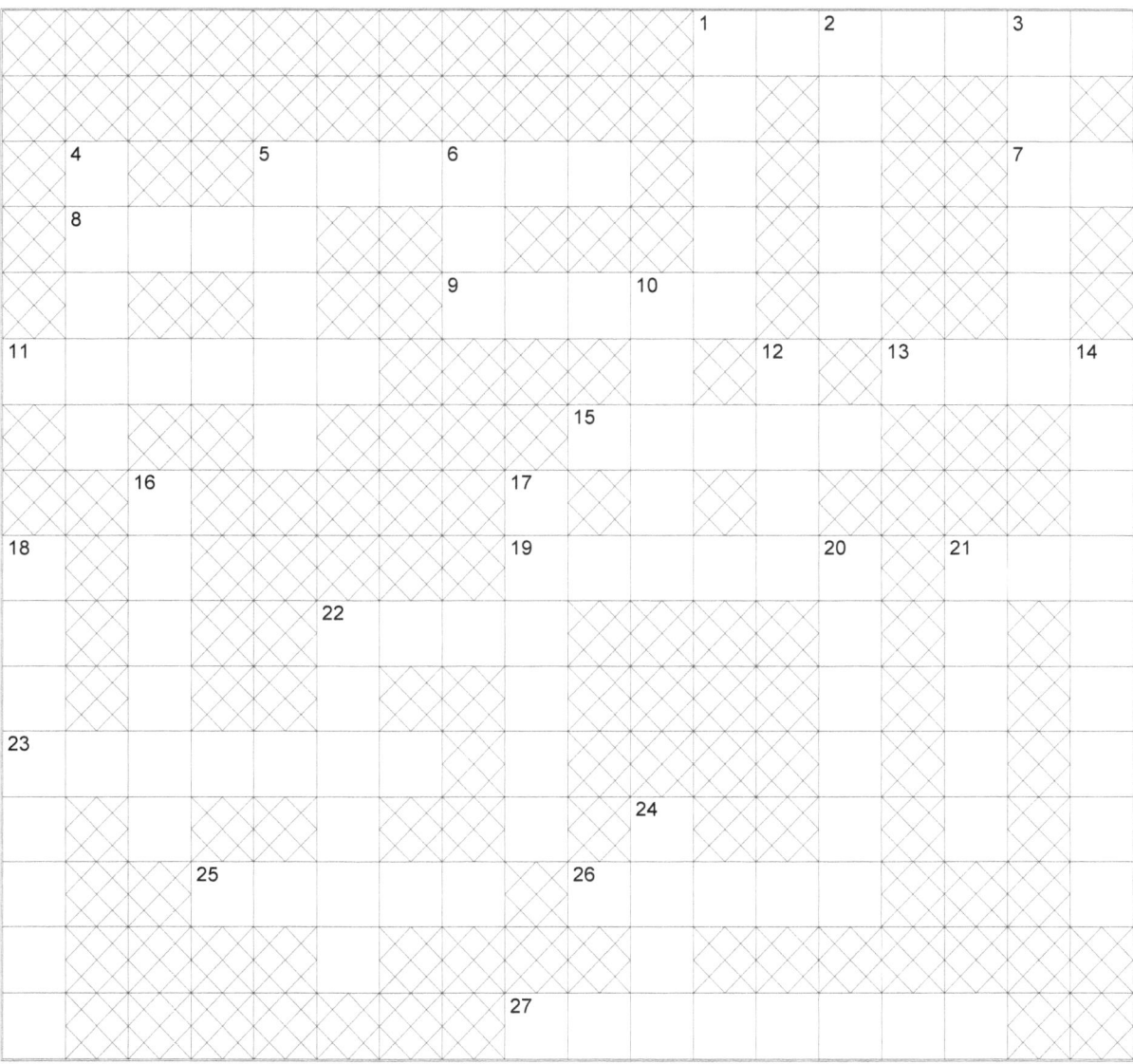

Across
1. Carlie compares one to her life; ___ machine
5. Mr. Mason told Thomas J about bumping Mr. Joe's ____
7. Harvey's birthday present
8. Classes Harvey's mother took
9. Benson twins don't believe in it
11. What Carlie wants to use on the bad memories
13. Funny present for Harvey's puppy; ____ pills
15. Book Benson twins gave Thomas J; Big ___ Stories
19. Month of birthday for Carlie and Thomas J
21. Number of stepfathers Carlie has
22. Carlie's favorite stars; Sonny and _____
23. Carlie learned to sew these
25. Gift from twins to Thomas J; gold ___
26. Harvey has two of these
27. Where Thomas J went with Mr. Mason

Down
1. Gift Thomas J and Carlie gave Harvey
2. Vocation Carlie has chosen; Good Luck ____
3. What Carlie hoped would come from her mother
4. Author
5. Benson twins' jewelry
6. Food to which Harvey was addicted
10. Carlie's Number One Rule as a nurse; No ___
12. Place Harvey's dad wanted to go
14. Carlie couldn't be one due to bad grades
16. Carlie wanted to put them on Harvey's toes
17. Where Thomas J went for a real haircut
18. Harvey's mother's new name at the commune
20. Second twin to die
21. Had article about Harvey's mother; New York ___
22. Teenage girl sent to foster home
24. Benson twins' favorite TV show; Tony Orlando & ___

Pinballs Crossword 1 Answer Key

							¹P	²I	N	²B	A	³L
							U		U			E
⁴B		⁵C	A	S	⁶K	E	T		P	R		⁷T	V
	⁸Y	O	G	A		F			P		S		T
		A		M		⁹C	A	N	¹⁰D	Y		E		E
¹¹E	R	A	S	E	R			Y		¹²E		¹³W	O	R	¹⁴M
	S			O			¹⁵B	I	B	L	E			A
			¹⁶D			¹⁷B		N		K				J
¹⁸B		E			¹⁹A	U	G	U	²⁰S		²¹T	W	O
E		C		²²C	H	E	R		H		I		R
T		A		H		B			O		M		E
²³H	A	L	T	E	R	S			M		E		T
E		S		L		R		²⁴D		A		S	T
N		²⁵C	O	I	N	S		²⁶C	A	S	T	S	E
I				E				W				
A				²⁷F	U	N	E	R	A	L	S	

Across
1. Carlie compares one to her life; ___ machine
5. Mr. Mason told Thomas J about bumping Mr. Joe's ___
7. Harvey's birthday present
8. Classes Harvey's mother took
9. Benson twins don't believe in it
11. What Carlie wants to use on the bad memories
13. Funny present for Harvey's puppy; ___ pills
15. Book Benson twins gave Thomas J; Big ___ Stories
19. Month of birthday for Carlie and Thomas J
21. Number of stepfathers Carlie has
22. Carlie's favorite stars; Sonny and _____
23. Carlie learned to sew these
25. Gift from twins to Thomas J; gold ___
26. Harvey has two of these
27. Where Thomas J went with Mr. Mason

Down
1. Gift Thomas J and Carlie gave Harvey
2. Vocation Carlie has chosen; Good Luck ___
3. What Carlie hoped would come from her mother
4. Author
5. Benson twins' jewelry
6. Food to which Harvey was addicted
10. Carlie's Number One Rule as a nurse; No ___
12. Place Harvey's dad wanted to go
14. Carlie couldn't be one due to bad grades
16. Carlie wanted to put them on Harvey's toes
17. Where Thomas J went for a real haircut
18. Harvey's mother's new name at the commune
20. Second twin to die
21. Had article about Harvey's mother; New York ___
22. Teenage girl sent to foster home
24. Benson twins' favorite TV show; Tony Orlando & ___

Pinballs Crossword 2

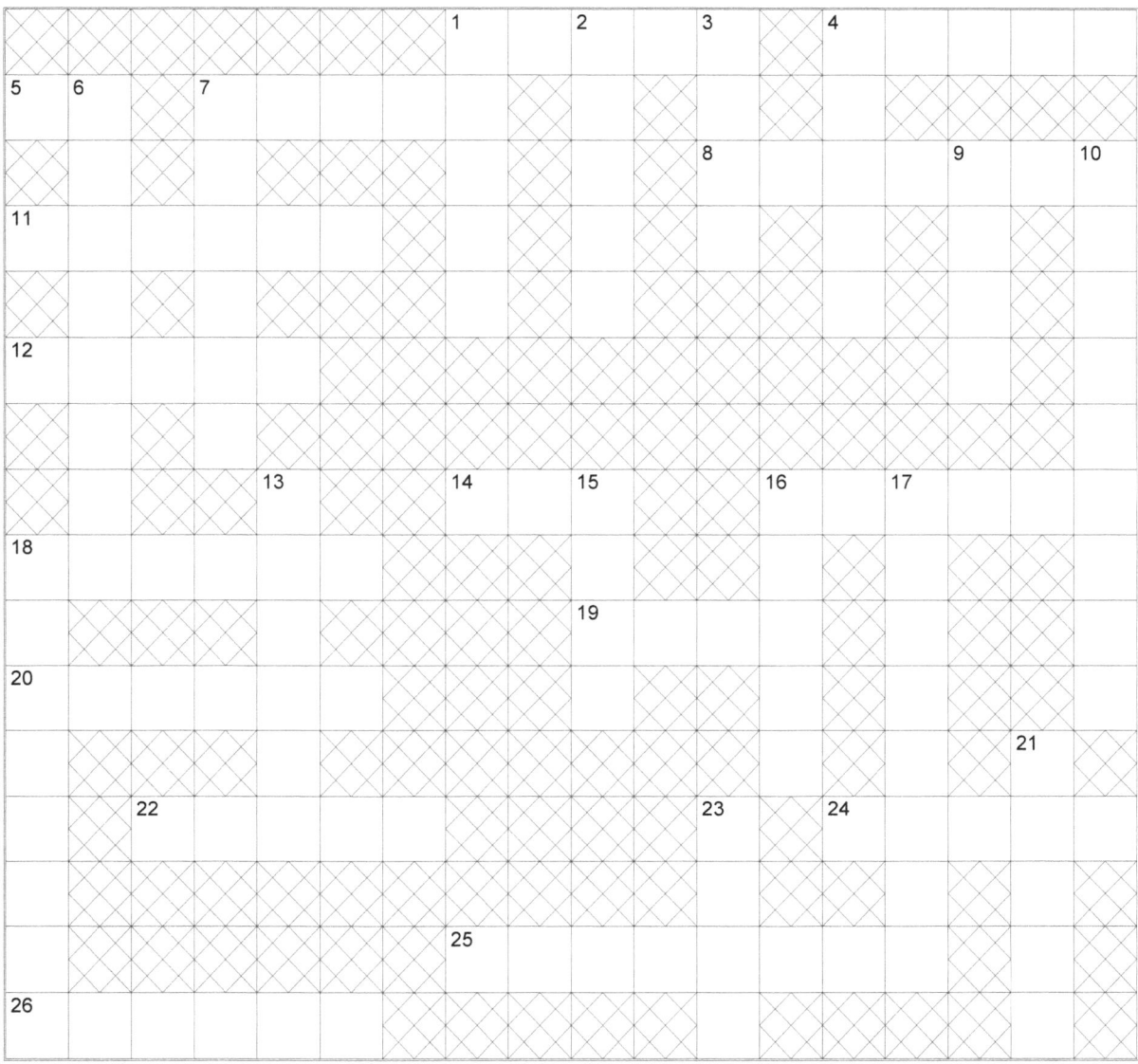

Across
1. Benson twins don't believe in it
4. Book Benson twins gave Thomas J; Big ___ Stories
5. Harvey's birthday present
7. Benson twins' jewelry
8. Harvey's dad's car
11. What Carlie wants to use on the bad memories
12. Had article about Harvey's mother; New York ___
14. Food to which Harvey was addicted
16. Teenage girl sent to foster home
18. Where Thomas J went for a real haircut
19. Place Harvey's dad wanted to go
20. Second twin to die
22. Harvey made these and learned about himself
24. Harvey's copy of his mother's article
25. Where Thomas J went with Mr. Mason
26. Month of birthday for Carlie and Thomas J

Down
1. Gift from twins to Thomas J; gold ___
2. Vocation Carlie has chosen; Good Luck ___
3. Classes Harvey's mother took
4. Author
6. Where Harvey's mother makes hammocks
7. Mr. Mason told Thomas J about bumping Mr. Joe's ___
9. Benson twins' favorite TV show; Tony Orlando & ___
10. Carlie couldn't be one due to bad grades
13. Carlie wanted to put them on Harvey's toes
15. Carlie's favorite stars; Sonny and _____
16. Harvey has two of these
17. Carlie's favorite show; Young and The ___
18. Harvey's mother's new name at the commune
21. Thomas J's favorite bible story; Baby ___
23. Funny present for Harvey's puppy; ___ pills

Pinballs Crossword 2 Answer Key

							1 C	2 A	3 N	D Y		4 B	I	B	L	E
5 T	6 V		7 C	A	M	E	O		U		O		Y			
	I		A				I		R		8 G	R	A	N	9 D	10 A M
11 E	R	A	S	E	R		N		S		A		R		A	J
	G		K				S		E		S		W		O	
12 T	I	M	E	S									N		R	
	N		T			13 D		14 K	F	15 C		16 C	17 A	R	L	I E
18 B	A	R	B	E	R			H		A		E			T	
E			C			19 E	L	K		S		S			T	
20 T	H	O	M	A	S			E	R			T			T	
H			L					S			L		21 M		E	
E		22 L	I	S	T	S				23 W		24 X	R	O	X	
N										O		S			S	
I					25 F	U	N	E	R	A	L	S			E	
26 A	U	G	U	S	T					M					S	

Across
1. Benson twins don't believe in it
4. Book Benson twins gave Thomas J; Big ___ Stories
5. Harvey's birthday present
7. Benson twins' jewelry
8. Harvey's dad's car
11. What Carlie wants to use on the bad memories
12. Had article about Harvey's mother; New York ___
14. Food to which Harvey was addicted
16. Teenage girl sent to foster home
18. Where Thomas J went for a real haircut
19. Place Harvey's dad wanted to go
20. Second twin to die
22. Harvey made these and learned about himself
24. Harvey's copy of his mother's article
25. Where Thomas J went with Mr. Mason
26. Month of birthday for Carlie and Thomas J

Down
1. Gift from twins to Thomas J; gold ___
2. Vocation Carlie has chosen; Good Luck ___
3. Classes Harvey's mother took
4. Author
6. Where Harvey's mother makes hammocks
7. Mr. Mason told Thomas J about bumping Mr. Joe's ___
9. Benson twins' favorite TV show; Tony Orlando & ___
10. Carlie couldn't be one due to bad grades
13. Carlie wanted to put them on Harvey's toes
15. Carlie's favorite stars; Sonny and _____
16. Harvey has two of these
17. Carlie's favorite show; Young and The ___
18. Harvey's mother's new name at the commune
21. Thomas J's favorite bible story; Baby ___
23. Funny present for Harvey's puppy; ____ pills

Pinballs Crossword 3

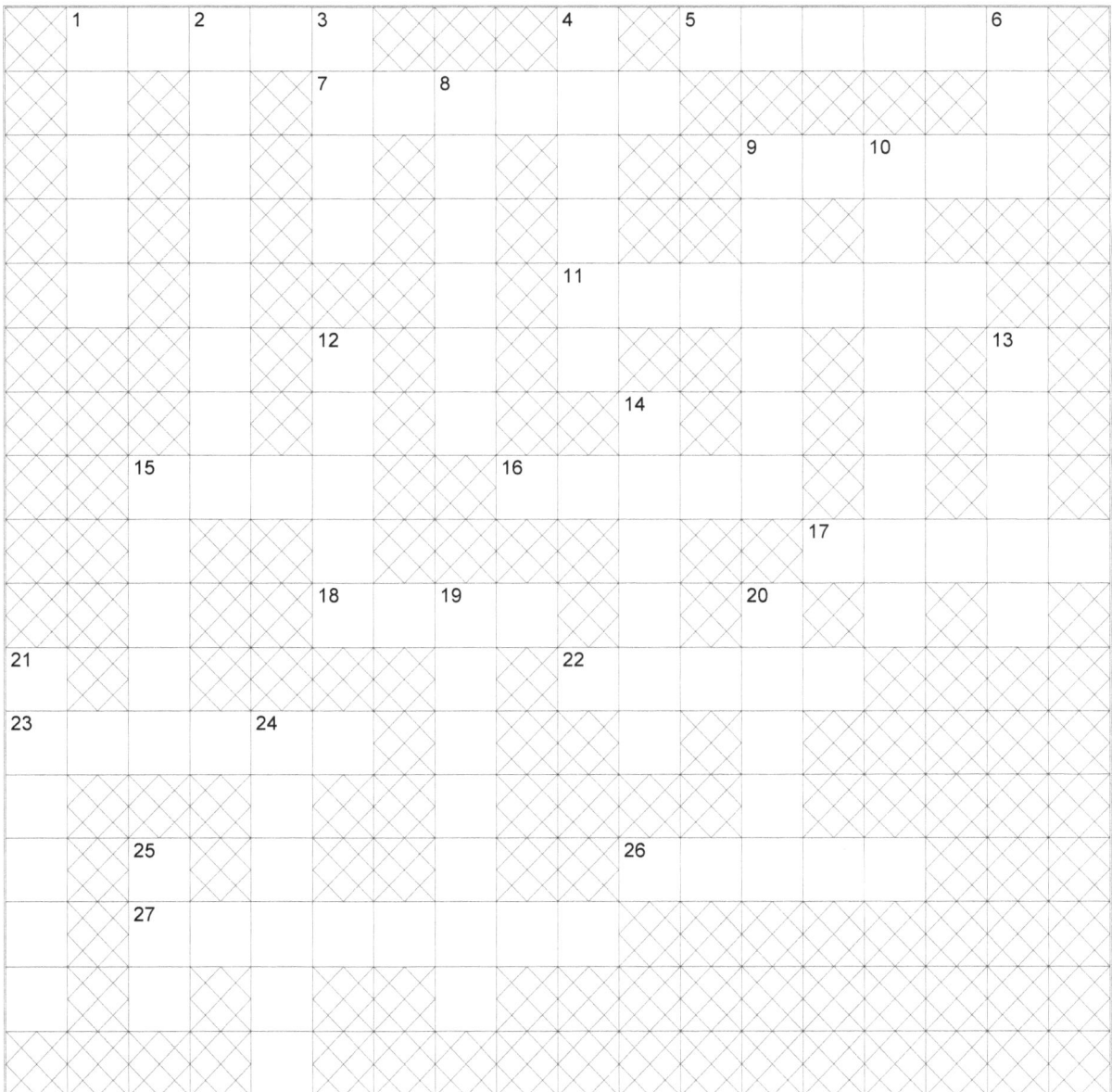

Across
1. Book Benson twins gave Thomas J; Big ___ Stories
5. Mr. Mason told Thomas J about bumping Mr. Joe's ___
7. What Carlie hoped would come from her mother
9. Benson twins' jewelry
11. Where Carlie takes Harvey in his wheelchair
15. Benson twins' favorite TV show; Tony Orlando & ___
16. Vocation Carlie has chosen; Good Luck ___
17. Harvey made these and learned about himself
18. Classes Harvey's mother took
22. Harvey's copy of his mother's article
23. Month of birthday for Carlie and Thomas J
26. Carlie, Thomas J, & Harvey's foster mother; Mrs. ___
27. How Harvey explains his broken legs; ___ injury

Down
1. Author
2. Harvey's mother's new name at the commune
3. Place Harvey's dad wanted to go
4. Carlie wanted to put them on Harvey's toes
6. Number of stepfathers Carlie has
8. Second twin to die
9. Teenage girl sent to foster home
10. Harvey's father drank these to forget
12. Benson twins don't believe in it
13. Harvey has two of these
14. What Carlie wants to use on the bad memories
15. Carlie's Number One Rule as a nurse; No ___
19. Harvey's dad's car
20. Gift from twins to Thomas J; gold ___
21. Where Thomas J went for a real haircut
24. Thomas wore a ___ t-shirt when dropped off
25. Food to which Harvey was addicted

Pinballs Crossword 3 Answer Key

	1 B	2 I	3 B	L	E		4 D		5 C	A	S	K	E	6 T	
	Y	E		7 L	8 E	T	T	E	R					W	
	A	T		K	H		C			9 C	A	10 M	E	O	
	R	H		S	O		A			A		A			
	S	E			M		11 L	I	B	R	A	R	Y		
		N		12 C	A		S			L		T		13 C	
		I		A		S		14 E		I		I		A	
		15 D	A	W	N		16 N	U	R	S	E		N	S	
		Y			D			A			17 L	I	S	T	S
				18 I	19 Y	O	G	A		20 C		S		S	
21 B		N			R		22 X	E	R	O	X				
23 A	U	G	U	24 S	T	A		R		I					
R				N		N				N					
B		25 K	O	D			26 M	A	S	O	N				
E		27 F	O	O	T	B	A	L	L						
R		C		P			M								
				Y											

Across
1. Book Benson twins gave Thomas J; Big ___ Stories
5. Mr. Mason told Thomas J about bumping Mr. Joe's ___
7. What Carlie hoped would come from her mother
9. Benson twins' jewelry
11. Where Carlie takes Harvey in his wheelchair
15. Benson twins' favorite TV show; Tony Orlando & ___
16. Vocation Carlie has chosen; Good Luck ___
17. Harvey made these and learned about himself
18. Classes Harvey's mother took
22. Harvey's copy of his mother's article
23. Month of birthday for Carlie and Thomas J
26. Carlie, Thomas J, & Harvey's foster mother; Mrs. ___
27. How Harvey explains his broken legs; ___ injury

Down
1. Author
2. Harvey's mother's new name at the commune
3. Place Harvey's dad wanted to go
4. Carlie wanted to put them on Harvey's toes
6. Number of stepfathers Carlie has
8. Second twin to die
9. Teenage girl sent to foster home
10. Harvey's father drank these to forget
12. Benson twins don't believe in it
13. Harvey has two of these
14. What Carlie wants to use on the bad memories
15. Carlie's Number One Rule as a nurse; No ___
19. Harvey's dad's car
20. Gift from twins to Thomas J; gold ___
21. Where Thomas J went for a real haircut
24. Thomas wore a ___ t-shirt when dropped off
25. Food to which Harvey was addicted

Pinballs Crossword 4

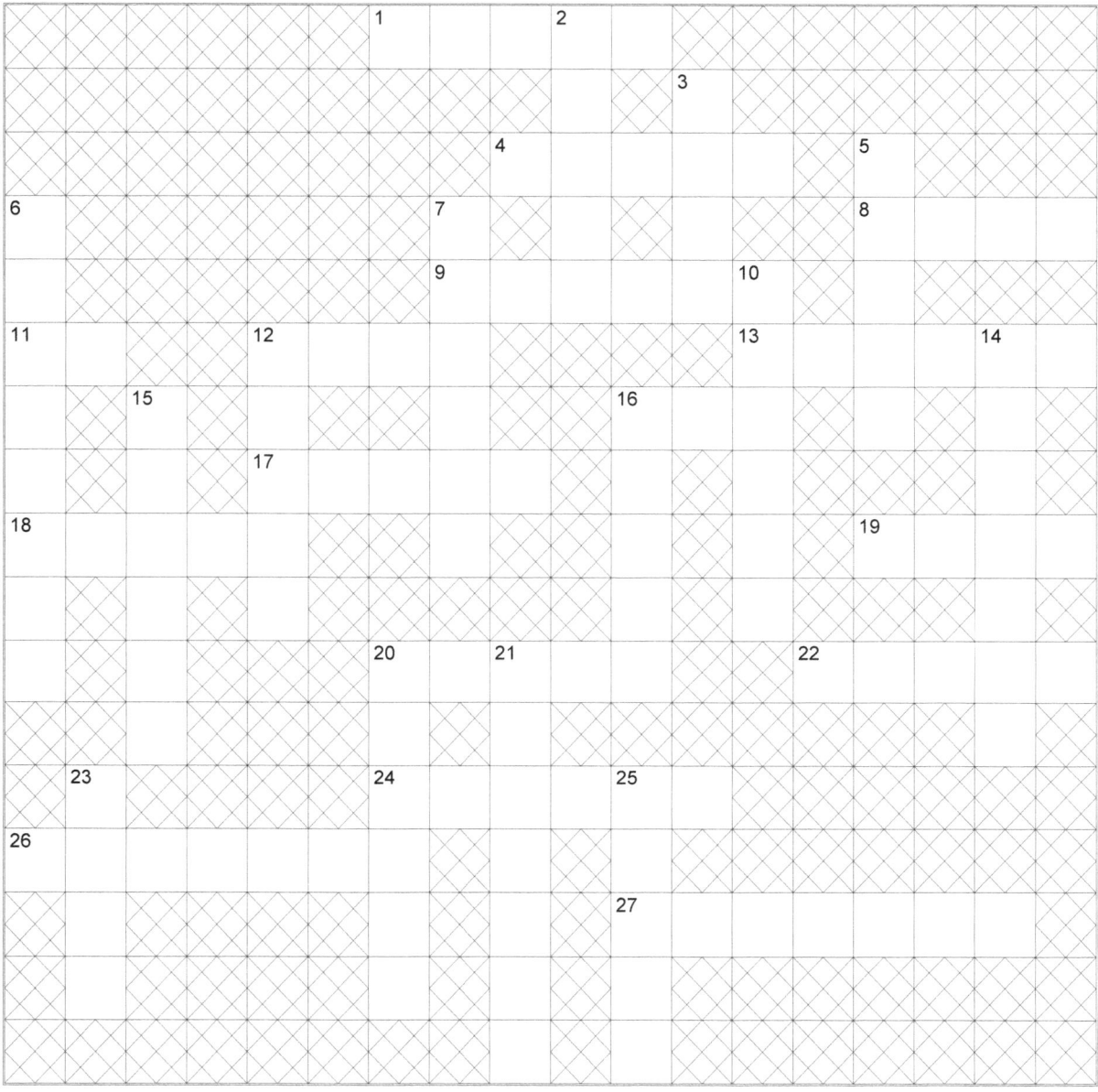

Across
1. Benson twins don't believe in it
4. Book Benson twins gave Thomas J; Big ___ Stories
8. Classes Harvey's mother took
9. Month of birthday for Carlie and Thomas J
11. Harvey's birthday present
12. Carlie's favorite stars; Sonny and _____
13. Boy with two legs in casts
16. Number of stepfathers Carlie has
17. Thomas J's favorite bible story; Baby ___
18. Vocation Carlie has chosen; Good Luck ____
19. Funny present for Harvey's puppy; ____ pills
20. Harvey has two of these
22. Gift from twins to Thomas J; gold ___
24. Thomas wore a ___ t-shirt when dropped off
26. Picture in article shows Harvey's mom making one
27. Carlie compares one to her life; ___ machine

Down
2. Carlie's Number One Rule as a nurse; No ___
3. Place Harvey's dad wanted to go
5. Author
6. Harvey's mother's new name at the commune
7. Where Thomas J went for a real haircut
10. Second twin to die
12. Benson twins' jewelry
14. Carlie lost this & Thomas J found it
15. Teenage girl sent to foster home
16. Had article about Harvey's mother; New York ___
20. Mr. Mason told Thomas J about bumping Mr. Joe's ____
21. How Thomas J spoke
23. Benson twins' favorite TV show; Tony Orlando & ___
25. Gift Thomas J and Carlie gave Harvey

Pinballs Crossword 4 Answer Key

					1 C	A	N	2 D	Y				
								Y		3 E			
					4 B	I	B	L	E		5 B		
6 B				7 B		N		K			8 Y	O	G A
E				9 A	U	G	U	S	T		10 A		
11 T	V		12 C	H	E	R			13 H	A	R	V	14 E Y
H		15 C	A		B		16 T	W	O		S		A
E		A	17 M	O	S	E	S		M				R
18 N	U	R	S	E		R		M			19 W	O	R M
I		L	O				E		S				I
A		I		20 C	A	21 S	T	S		22 C	O	I	N S
		E		A		H							G
23 D			24 S	N	O	O	25 P	Y					
26 H	A	M	M	O	C	K		U					
W			E			T		27 P	I	N	B	A	L L
N			T			E		P					
						D		Y					

Across
1. Benson twins don't believe in it
4. Book Benson twins gave Thomas J; Big ___ Stories
8. Classes Harvey's mother took
9. Month of birthday for Carlie and Thomas J
11. Harvey's birthday present
12. Carlie's favorite stars; Sonny and _____
13. Boy with two legs in casts
16. Number of stepfathers Carlie has
17. Thomas J's favorite bible story; Baby ___
18. Vocation Carlie has chosen;Good Luck ____
19. Funny present for Harvey's puppy; ____ pills
20. Harvey has two of these
22. Gift from twins to Thomas J; gold ___
24. Thomas wore a ___ t-shirt when dropped off
26. Picture in article shows Harvey's mom making one
27. Carlie compares one to her life; ___ machine

Down
2. Carlie's Number One Rule as a nurse; No ___
3. Place Harvey's dad wanted to go
5. Author
6. Harvey's mother's new name at the commune
7. Where Thomas J went for a real haircut
10. Second twin to die
12. Benson twins' jewelry
14. Carlie lost this & Thomas J found it
15. Teenage girl sent to foster home
16. Had article about Harvey's mother; New York ___
20. Mr. Mason told Thomas J about bumping Mr. Joe's ____
21. How Thomas J spoke
23. Benson twins' favorite TV show; Tony Orlando & ___
25. Gift Thomas J and Carlie gave Harvey

Pinballs

LIBRARY	PUPPY	PINBALLS	TWO	KFC
PINBALL	EARRING	DECORETTES	SHOUTED	HALTERS
COINS	DAWN	FREE SPACE	THOMAS	ELKS
MAYONNAISE	RESTLESS	DECALS	TIMES	MASON
CASKET	CASTS	FUNERALS	SNOOPY	GRANDAM

Pinballs

WORM	HAMMOCK	BYARS	AUGUST	MOSES
CAMEO	LISTS	JEFFERSON	CANDY	MAJORETTE
BETHENIA	XEROX	FREE SPACE	ERASER	NURSE
CHER	SNOWBALL	LETTER	HARVEY	BARBER
FOOTBALL	VIRGINIA	DYING	CONSTRUCTION	YOGA

Pinballs

JEFFERSON	ERASER	RESTLESS	COINS	EARRING
CONSTRUCTION	VIRGINIA	DAWN	CHER	ELKS
AUGUST	LIBRARY	FREE SPACE	HAMMOCK	SHOUTED
HALTERS	LISTS	FOOTBALL	PUPPY	PINBALL
MAYONNAISE	KFC	TV	MAJORETTE	HARVEY

Pinballs

BIBLE	BYARS	CASKET	SNOWBALL	BETHENIA
YOGA	NURSE	MASON	MARTINIS	SNOOPY
CANDY	MOSES	FREE SPACE	WORM	DECALS
BARBER	CASTS	TWO	XEROX	DECORETTES
LETTER	GRANDAM	CARLIE	THOMAS	CAMEO

Pinballs

EARRING	BIBLE	WORM	TV	LISTS
CASTS	LIBRARY	MARTINIS	FOOTBALL	VIRGINIA
SNOOPY	AUGUST	FREE SPACE	DECORETTES	PUPPY
COINS	CARLIE	BYARS	MOSES	SHOUTED
CHER	HALTERS	NURSE	JEFFERSON	BETHENIA

Pinballs

CONSTRUCTION	LETTER	PINBALL	HARVEY	ERASER
ELKS	CANDY	MAYONNAISE	FUNERALS	DAWN
PINBALLS	MASON	FREE SPACE	TWO	RESTLESS
CAMEO	DECALS	CASKET	BARBER	GRANDAM
MAJORETTE	SNOWBALL	YOGA	TIMES	KFC

Pinballs

BYARS	JEFFERSON	FUNERALS	CARLIE	LETTER
TWO	SNOWBALL	SHOUTED	XEROX	CASKET
NURSE	GRANDAM	FREE SPACE	SNOOPY	DECALS
TIMES	THOMAS	BARBER	RESTLESS	LIBRARY
CAMEO	COINS	BIBLE	KFC	DYING

Pinballs

MAJORETTE	AUGUST	HAMMOCK	EARRING	CONSTRUCTION
FOOTBALL	DAWN	TV	DECORETTES	MAYONNAISE
PINBALLS	ELKS	FREE SPACE	CHER	MASON
CASTS	PUPPY	MOSES	CANDY	VIRGINIA
WORM	YOGA	HARVEY	PINBALL	ERASER

48
Copyrighted

Pinballs

HAMMOCK	DYING	CAMEO	AUGUST	HARVEY
MARTINIS	VIRGINIA	CARLIE	MOSES	GRANDAM
BIBLE	ELKS	FREE SPACE	DECALS	SNOOPY
PINBALLS	LIBRARY	YOGA	HALTERS	KFC
NURSE	BARBER	DAWN	COINS	XEROX

Pinballs

CONSTRUCTION	FUNERALS	TIMES	RESTLESS	BETHENIA
PUPPY	DECORETTES	LISTS	WORM	PINBALL
FOOTBALL	MASON	FREE SPACE	TWO	BYARS
EARRING	LETTER	SHOUTED	CASKET	MAJORETTE
CHER	MAYONNAISE	CASTS	TV	ERASER

Pinballs

CONSTRUCTION	KFC	WORM	CANDY	DECORETTES
RESTLESS	VIRGINIA	YOGA	PINBALL	CAMEO
COINS	PUPPY	FREE SPACE	TWO	LISTS
XEROX	CASKET	SNOWBALL	EARRING	MASON
ELKS	TV	HAMMOCK	HARVEY	GRANDAM

Pinballs

BETHENIA	FUNERALS	TIMES	MARTINIS	DYING
HALTERS	BIBLE	BYARS	THOMAS	PINBALLS
CASTS	LIBRARY	FREE SPACE	SHOUTED	ERASER
CARLIE	NURSE	LETTER	MAJORETTE	SNOOPY
AUGUST	DECALS	MOSES	CHER	MAYONNAISE

Pinballs

EARRING	XEROX	MASON	BIBLE	CARLIE
CONSTRUCTION	DYING	BETHENIA	CAMEO	GRANDAM
DAWN	TWO	FREE SPACE	BARBER	ELKS
BYARS	YOGA	VIRGINIA	HARVEY	COINS
DECORETTES	SHOUTED	TV	SNOOPY	MAJORETTE

Pinballs

MOSES	HAMMOCK	RESTLESS	HALTERS	FUNERALS
CANDY	MAYONNAISE	SNOWBALL	FOOTBALL	LETTER
THOMAS	CASKET	FREE SPACE	WORM	MARTINIS
CASTS	KFC	PUPPY	PINBALL	TIMES
LIBRARY	DECALS	AUGUST	JEFFERSON	LISTS

Pinballs

FUNERALS	TWO	TV	AUGUST	DAWN
XEROX	BARBER	ERASER	SNOWBALL	RESTLESS
CANDY	CAMEO	FREE SPACE	DECALS	MASON
GRANDAM	LETTER	PUPPY	EARRING	LISTS
HALTERS	DECORETTES	CARLIE	MARTINIS	LIBRARY

Pinballs

PINBALL	COINS	PINBALLS	JEFFERSON	SNOOPY
MOSES	NURSE	HAMMOCK	WORM	VIRGINIA
KFC	BETHENIA	FREE SPACE	FOOTBALL	CHER
CONSTRUCTION	HARVEY	BYARS	CASKET	MAJORETTE
BIBLE	THOMAS	MAYONNAISE	ELKS	TIMES

Pinballs

NURSE	CARLIE	AUGUST	PUPPY	BYARS
DYING	SNOWBALL	WORM	BARBER	DECORETTES
THOMAS	COINS	FREE SPACE	CASTS	CHER
MAJORETTE	YOGA	TV	GRANDAM	SNOOPY
LIBRARY	BETHENIA	XEROX	CONSTRUCTION	HARVEY

Pinballs

BIBLE	PINBALL	ELKS	SHOUTED	LETTER
CAMEO	HALTERS	MOSES	FUNERALS	DECALS
ERASER	JEFFERSON	FREE SPACE	HAMMOCK	MASON
TWO	VIRGINIA	MAYONNAISE	LISTS	CASKET
MARTINIS	RESTLESS	EARRING	TIMES	FOOTBALL

Pinballs

ELKS	FUNERALS	MOSES	CASTS	DECORETTES
HAMMOCK	MARTINIS	WORM	MAJORETTE	YOGA
NURSE	HARVEY	FREE SPACE	COINS	LISTS
TWO	KFC	DAWN	SNOWBALL	SNOOPY
FOOTBALL	DECALS	MAYONNAISE	BARBER	TV

Pinballs

SHOUTED	LETTER	BETHENIA	THOMAS	CASKET
PINBALL	PINBALLS	RESTLESS	BIBLE	CHER
XEROX	JEFFERSON	FREE SPACE	EARRING	VIRGINIA
GRANDAM	CARLIE	MASON	PUPPY	DYING
TIMES	BYARS	CONSTRUCTION	CAMEO	AUGUST

Pinballs

MAYONNAISE	HAMMOCK	BETHENIA	SNOWBALL	MASON
THOMAS	LIBRARY	DECORETTES	WORM	PUPPY
CANDY	MOSES	FREE SPACE	DECALS	SNOOPY
CASKET	MARTINIS	FOOTBALL	TWO	MAJORETTE
CHER	JEFFERSON	CARLIE	PINBALL	ERASER

Pinballs

HALTERS	KFC	DYING	DAWN	EARRING
GRANDAM	FUNERALS	CONSTRUCTION	TV	LETTER
YOGA	TIMES	FREE SPACE	AUGUST	XEROX
BYARS	NURSE	VIRGINIA	CASTS	BARBER
SHOUTED	RESTLESS	ELKS	PINBALLS	HARVEY

Pinballs

MOSES	TIMES	MARTINIS	BIBLE	VIRGINIA
MAYONNAISE	PUPPY	DYING	EARRING	CARLIE
CHER	AUGUST	FREE SPACE	MASON	FUNERALS
HALTERS	TWO	WORM	HAMMOCK	BARBER
DECALS	PINBALLS	HARVEY	ELKS	KFC

Pinballs

FOOTBALL	JEFFERSON	TV	CONSTRUCTION	SNOWBALL
COINS	XEROX	MAJORETTE	YOGA	LIBRARY
DAWN	SHOUTED	FREE SPACE	PINBALL	SNOOPY
CASTS	LISTS	CAMEO	BETHENIA	BYARS
CANDY	GRANDAM	THOMAS	NURSE	RESTLESS

Pinballs

PINBALLS	FOOTBALL	MASON	VIRGINIA	SNOOPY
TV	BETHENIA	MAJORETTE	HAMMOCK	BIBLE
AUGUST	YOGA	FREE SPACE	TWO	PUPPY
BYARS	MAYONNAISE	WORM	CHER	ELKS
EARRING	SHOUTED	FUNERALS	PINBALL	DAWN

Pinballs

HARVEY	JEFFERSON	GRANDAM	SNOWBALL	MARTINIS
THOMAS	CANDY	XEROX	MOSES	DYING
CARLIE	DECORETTES	FREE SPACE	COINS	LETTER
ERASER	CASKET	LISTS	NURSE	CONSTRUCTION
KFC	HALTERS	TIMES	RESTLESS	LIBRARY

Pinballs

HARVEY	FOOTBALL	LIBRARY	PINBALL	HAMMOCK
PUPPY	THOMAS	LISTS	FUNERALS	WORM
SHOUTED	AUGUST	FREE SPACE	MARTINIS	DECORETTES
SNOWBALL	BYARS	HALTERS	KFC	MAJORETTE
YOGA	PINBALLS	VIRGINIA	CARLIE	MOSES

Pinballs

SNOOPY	COINS	XEROX	CONSTRUCTION	CHER
TV	DAWN	LETTER	NURSE	CASTS
BETHENIA	CAMEO	FREE SPACE	MASON	TWO
TIMES	JEFFERSON	RESTLESS	MAYONNAISE	DECALS
BARBER	GRANDAM	CASKET	DYING	ERASER

Pinballs

AUGUST	SNOOPY	KFC	NURSE	FUNERALS
DECALS	TWO	ERASER	THOMAS	CASKET
PINBALLS	JEFFERSON	FREE SPACE	WORM	MASON
BETHENIA	TIMES	CHER	PUPPY	CONSTRUCTION
ELKS	HARVEY	LETTER	BYARS	PINBALL

Pinballs

FOOTBALL	CAMEO	HALTERS	MAJORETTE	CARLIE
LIBRARY	YOGA	CANDY	TV	MAYONNAISE
DYING	LISTS	FREE SPACE	EARRING	SNOWBALL
RESTLESS	SHOUTED	COINS	MOSES	GRANDAM
DAWN	HAMMOCK	XEROX	BARBER	MARTINIS

Pinballs

CHER	EARRING	HARVEY	MARTINIS	VIRGINIA
PUPPY	AUGUST	JEFFERSON	HALTERS	LISTS
BETHENIA	MAYONNAISE	FREE SPACE	FUNERALS	THOMAS
FOOTBALL	SNOOPY	PINBALL	RESTLESS	CASTS
SNOWBALL	BIBLE	MOSES	DECALS	NURSE

Pinballs

CASKET	ERASER	SHOUTED	XEROX	CARLIE
LIBRARY	TWO	DAWN	MASON	GRANDAM
ELKS	TV	FREE SPACE	TIMES	COINS
CAMEO	WORM	HAMMOCK	PINBALLS	MAJORETTE
CANDY	KFC	BARBER	YOGA	BYARS

Pinballs Vocabulary Word List

No.	Word	Clue/Definition
1.	ADMIRATION	Respect
2.	ADOPTIVE	Related by adoption
3.	AGONIZED	Tormented over
4.	APPALACHIAN	Referring to that area of mountains in the eastern U.S.
5.	APPEALED	Attracted
6.	APPENDECTOMY	Operation to remove appendix
7.	ASTONISHED	Shocked
8.	BLURT	Shout
9.	BOUTIQUE	Specialty shop
10.	CLAMPED	Tightly closed
11.	CLENCHED	With jaws tightly closed
12.	COFFIN	Casket; box in which to bury dead person
13.	COMMOTION	Excitement
14.	COMMUNE	Community where people live and work cooperatively
15.	COMPLIMENTS	To show kindness by a gift
16.	CONCUSSION	Swelling from a blow
17.	CONTRACT	Written agreement
18.	DISGUSTED	Repulsed
19.	DREAD	Great fear
20.	EARNESTLY	Sincerely
21.	ESTABLISHED	Founded
22.	FIDGET	Squirm
23.	FORGE	Fake
24.	GNARLED	Twisted
25.	HALTER	Short top that ties behind the neck and across the back
26.	HOVERED	Lingered
27.	HUNCHED	Bent
28.	HYPODERMIC	Needle used under the skin
29.	INCISIONS	Cuts
30.	INSULT	Offend
31.	JARRED	Bumped
32.	MINE	A quarry or well
33.	PITIFUL	Pathetic
34.	REFLECTION	Likeness; mirror image
35.	RESEMBLED	Looked like
36.	RESENTED	Disliked; took exception to for some reason
37.	RESPECTFULLY	Politely
38.	RHYTHMIC	Having a steady motion
39.	SHRIVELED	Withered
40.	SPIGOT	Faucet
41.	SQUINTED	Partly closed eyes; in question
42.	STABILIZES	Calms down
43.	SULKING	Moping
44.	SUMMONED	Called; requested
45.	SUPERIOR	Snobbish; better than others
46.	SUSPICION	Distrust
47.	UNCOMPLIMENTARY	Negative
48.	VACCINES	Preventative shots
49.	VIRUSES	Infections

Pinballs Vocabulary Fill In The Blank 1

_____ 1. Calms down

_____ 2. Shout

_____ 3. Written agreement

_____ 4. Infections

_____ 5. Fake

_____ 6. Politely

_____ 7. Moping

_____ 8. Bumped

_____ 9. Snobbish; better than others

_____ 10. With jaws tightly closed

_____ 11. Tightly closed

_____ 12. Lingered

_____ 13. Twisted

_____ 14. Disliked; took exception to for some reason

_____ 15. Community where people live and work cooperatively

_____ 16. Withered

_____ 17. Pathetic

_____ 18. Bent

_____ 19. Needle used under the skin

_____ 20. Shocked

Pinballs Vocabulary Fill In The Blank 1 Answer Key

STABILIZES	1. Calms down
BLURT	2. Shout
CONTRACT	3. Written agreement
VIRUSES	4. Infections
FORGE	5. Fake
RESPECTFULLY	6. Politely
SULKING	7. Moping
JARRED	8. Bumped
SUPERIOR	9. Snobbish; better than others
CLENCHED	10. With jaws tightly closed
CLAMPED	11. Tightly closed
HOVERED	12. Lingered
GNARLED	13. Twisted
RESENTED	14. Disliked; took exception to for some reason
COMMUNE	15. Community where people live and work cooperatively
SHRIVELED	16. Withered
PITIFUL	17. Pathetic
HUNCHED	18. Bent
HYPODERMIC	19. Needle used under the skin
ASTONISHED	20. Shocked

Pinballs Vocabulary Fill In The Blank 2

_____ 1. Community where people live and work cooperatively

_____ 2. Swelling from a blow

_____ 3. Excitement

_____ 4. Lingered

_____ 5. Looked like

_____ 6. Great fear

_____ 7. Tightly closed

_____ 8. A quarry or well

_____ 9. Twisted

_____ 10. Moping

_____ 11. Faucet

_____ 12. Repulsed

_____ 13. Squirm

_____ 14. Negative

_____ 15. Partly closed eyes; in question

_____ 16. Snobbish; better than others

_____ 17. Casket; box in which to bury dead person

_____ 18. Bumped

_____ 19. Bent

_____ 20. Cuts

Pinballs Vocabulary Fill In The Blank 2 Answer Key

COMMUNE	1. Community where people live and work cooperatively
CONCUSSION	2. Swelling from a blow
COMMOTION	3. Excitement
HOVERED	4. Lingered
RESEMBLED	5. Looked like
DREAD	6. Great fear
CLAMPED	7. Tightly closed
MINE	8. A quarry or well
GNARLED	9. Twisted
SULKING	10. Moping
SPIGOT	11. Faucet
DISGUSTED	12. Repulsed
FIDGET	13. Squirm
UNCOMPLIMENTARY	14. Negative
SQUINTED	15. Partly closed eyes; in question
SUPERIOR	16. Snobbish; better than others
COFFIN	17. Casket; box in which to bury dead person
JARRED	18. Bumped
HUNCHED	19. Bent
INCISIONS	20. Cuts

Pinballs Vocabulary Fill In The Blank 3

_____ 1. Called; requested

_____ 2. Lingered

_____ 3. With jaws tightly closed

_____ 4. Having a steady motion

_____ 5. Calms down

_____ 6. To show kindness by a gift

_____ 7. Politely

_____ 8. Infections

_____ 9. Operation to remove appendix

_____ 10. Pathetic

_____ 11. Short top that ties behind the neck and across the back

_____ 12. Likeness; mirror image

_____ 13. Negative

_____ 14. Founded

_____ 15. Offend

_____ 16. Needle used under the skin

_____ 17. Excitement

_____ 18. Fake

_____ 19. Twisted

_____ 20. Cuts

Pinballs Vocabulary Fill In The Blank 3 Answer Key

SUMMONED	1. Called; requested
HOVERED	2. Lingered
CLENCHED	3. With jaws tightly closed
RHYTHMIC	4. Having a steady motion
STABILIZES	5. Calms down
COMPLIMENTS	6. To show kindness by a gift
RESPECTFULLY	7. Politely
VIRUSES	8. Infections
APPENDECTOMY	9. Operation to remove appendix
PITIFUL	10. Pathetic
HALTER	11. Short top that ties behind the neck and across the back
REFLECTION	12. Likeness; mirror image
UNCOMPLIMENTARY	13. Negative
ESTABLISHED	14. Founded
INSULT	15. Offend
HYPODERMIC	16. Needle used under the skin
COMMOTION	17. Excitement
FORGE	18. Fake
GNARLED	19. Twisted
INCISIONS	20. Cuts

Pinballs Vocabulary Fill In The Blank 4

_____ 1. Politely

_____ 2. Community where people live and work cooperatively

_____ 3. Preventative shots

_____ 4. Repulsed

_____ 5. Operation to remove appendix

_____ 6. Offend

_____ 7. Negative

_____ 8. Pathetic

_____ 9. Casket; box in which to bury dead person

_____ 10. Referring to that area of mountains in the eastern U.S.

_____ 11. Twisted

_____ 12. Related by adoption

_____ 13. Swelling from a blow

_____ 14. Excitement

_____ 15. Shocked

_____ 16. Specialty shop

_____ 17. Having a steady motion

_____ 18. Called; requested

_____ 19. Snobbish; better than others

_____ 20. Looked like

Pinballs Vocabulary Fill In The Blank 4 Answer Key

RESPECTFULLY	1. Politely
COMMUNE	2. Community where people live and work cooperatively
VACCINES	3. Preventative shots
DISGUSTED	4. Repulsed
APPENDECTOMY	5. Operation to remove appendix
INSULT	6. Offend
UNCOMPLIMENTARY	7. Negative
PITIFUL	8. Pathetic
COFFIN	9. Casket; box in which to bury dead person
APPALACHIAN	10. Referring to that area of mountains in the eastern U.S.
GNARLED	11. Twisted
ADOPTIVE	12. Related by adoption
CONCUSSION	13. Swelling from a blow
COMMOTION	14. Excitement
ASTONISHED	15. Shocked
BOUTIQUE	16. Specialty shop
RHYTHMIC	17. Having a steady motion
SUMMONED	18. Called; requested
SUPERIOR	19. Snobbish; better than others
RESEMBLED	20. Looked like

Pinballs Vocabulary Matching 1

___ 1. INSULT   A. Disliked; took exception to for some reason
___ 2. CONCUSSION   B. Respect
___ 3. ADOPTIVE   C. Attracted
___ 4. ADMIRATION   D. Referring to that area of mountains in the eastern U.S.
___ 5. UNCOMPLIMENTARY   E. Twisted
___ 6. VACCINES   F. Pathetic
___ 7. ESTABLISHED   G. Preventative shots
___ 8. DREAD   H. Short top that ties behind the neck and across the back
___ 9. CLAMPED   I. Tightly closed
___10. HALTER   J. Swelling from a blow
___11. RESPECTFULLY   K. Bent
___12. DISGUSTED   L. Offend
___13. SUPERIOR   M. Related by adoption
___14. CLENCHED   N. Withered
___15. RESENTED   O. Squirm
___16. REFLECTION   P. Likeness; mirror image
___17. BLURT   Q. Repulsed
___18. FIDGET   R. Shout
___19. COMMOTION   S. Negative
___20. APPALACHIAN   T. Founded
___21. SHRIVELED   U. Snobbish; better than others
___22. PITIFUL   V. Politely
___23. HUNCHED   W. Excitement
___24. APPEALED   X. With jaws tightly closed
___25. GNARLED   Y. Great fear

Pinballs Vocabulary Matching 1 Answer Key

L -	1. INSULT	A. Disliked; took exception to for some reason
J -	2. CONCUSSION	B. Respect
M -	3. ADOPTIVE	C. Attracted
B -	4. ADMIRATION	D. Referring to that area of mountains in the eastern U.S.
S -	5. UNCOMPLIMENTARY	E. Twisted
G -	6. VACCINES	F. Pathetic
T -	7. ESTABLISHED	G. Preventative shots
Y -	8. DREAD	H. Short top that ties behind the neck and across the back
I -	9. CLAMPED	I. Tightly closed
H -	10. HALTER	J. Swelling from a blow
V -	11. RESPECTFULLY	K. Bent
Q -	12. DISGUSTED	L. Offend
U -	13. SUPERIOR	M. Related by adoption
X -	14. CLENCHED	N. Withered
A -	15. RESENTED	O. Squirm
P -	16. REFLECTION	P. Likeness; mirror image
R -	17. BLURT	Q. Repulsed
O -	18. FIDGET	R. Shout
W -	19. COMMOTION	S. Negative
D -	20. APPALACHIAN	T. Founded
N -	21. SHRIVELED	U. Snobbish; better than others
F -	22. PITIFUL	V. Politely
K -	23. HUNCHED	W. Excitement
C -	24. APPEALED	X. With jaws tightly closed
E -	25. GNARLED	Y. Great fear

Pinballs Vocabulary Matching 2

___ 1. HUNCHED   A. Community where people live and work cooperatively
___ 2. ADMIRATION   B. Squirm
___ 3. REFLECTION   C. Bumped
___ 4. CONTRACT   D. Respect
___ 5. HOVERED   E. Founded
___ 6. ESTABLISHED   F. Shout
___ 7. JARRED   G. Called; requested
___ 8. HALTER   H. Likeness; mirror image
___ 9. RHYTHMIC   I. Related by adoption
___10. APPALACHIAN   J. Specialty shop
___11. BLURT   K. Referring to that area of mountains in the eastern U.S.
___12. SUSPICION   L. Cuts
___13. FIDGET   M. Tormented over
___14. COMMOTION   N. Written agreement
___15. COMMUNE   O. Lingered
___16. AGONIZED   P. Shocked
___17. CONCUSSION   Q. Distrust
___18. ASTONISHED   R. Excitement
___19. SQUINTED   S. Swelling from a blow
___20. BOUTIQUE   T. Bent
___21. MINE   U. Short top that ties behind the neck and across the back
___22. INCISIONS   V. Having a steady motion
___23. ADOPTIVE   W. A quarry or well
___24. SUMMONED   X. Partly closed eyes; in question
___25. EARNESTLY   Y. Sincerely

Pinballs Vocabulary Matching 2 Answer Key

T - 1. HUNCHED	A.	Community where people live and work cooperatively
D - 2. ADMIRATION	B.	Squirm
H - 3. REFLECTION	C.	Bumped
N - 4. CONTRACT	D.	Respect
O - 5. HOVERED	E.	Founded
E - 6. ESTABLISHED	F.	Shout
C - 7. JARRED	G.	Called; requested
U - 8. HALTER	H.	Likeness; mirror image
V - 9. RHYTHMIC	I.	Related by adoption
K - 10. APPALACHIAN	J.	Specialty shop
F - 11. BLURT	K.	Referring to that area of mountains in the eastern U.S.
Q - 12. SUSPICION	L.	Cuts
B - 13. FIDGET	M.	Tormented over
R - 14. COMMOTION	N.	Written agreement
A - 15. COMMUNE	O.	Lingered
M - 16. AGONIZED	P.	Shocked
S - 17. CONCUSSION	Q.	Distrust
P - 18. ASTONISHED	R.	Excitement
X - 19. SQUINTED	S.	Swelling from a blow
J - 20. BOUTIQUE	T.	Bent
W - 21. MINE	U.	Short top that ties behind the neck and across the back
L - 22. INCISIONS	V.	Having a steady motion
I - 23. ADOPTIVE	W.	A quarry or well
G - 24. SUMMONED	X.	Partly closed eyes; in question
Y - 25. EARNESTLY	Y.	Sincerely

Pinballs Vocabulary Matching 3

___ 1. COFFIN   A. Casket; box in which to bury dead person
___ 2. ADMIRATION   B. Shocked
___ 3. JARRED   C. Bumped
___ 4. SQUINTED   D. Shout
___ 5. RESENTED   E. Swelling from a blow
___ 6. CONTRACT   F. Excitement
___ 7. CONCUSSION   G. Called; requested
___ 8. RESEMBLED   H. Partly closed eyes; in question
___ 9. BLURT   I. Moping
___10. VIRUSES   J. Squirm
___11. DREAD   K. Calms down
___12. APPALACHIAN   L. Pathetic
___13. COMPLIMENTS   M. Referring to that area of mountains in the eastern U.S.
___14. ASTONISHED   N. Respect
___15. AGONIZED   O. Great fear
___16. SULKING   P. Tormented over
___17. FIDGET   Q. To show kindness by a gift
___18. GNARLED   R. Written agreement
___19. SHRIVELED   S. Fake
___20. PITIFUL   T. Looked like
___21. SUMMONED   U. Lingered
___22. FORGE   V. Withered
___23. COMMOTION   W. Twisted
___24. STABILIZES   X. Disliked; took exception to for some reason
___25. HOVERED   Y. Infections

Pinballs Vocabulary Matching 3 Answer Key

A - 1.	COFFIN	A.	Casket; box in which to bury dead person
N - 2.	ADMIRATION	B.	Shocked
C - 3.	JARRED	C.	Bumped
H - 4.	SQUINTED	D.	Shout
X - 5.	RESENTED	E.	Swelling from a blow
R - 6.	CONTRACT	F.	Excitement
E - 7.	CONCUSSION	G.	Called; requested
T - 8.	RESEMBLED	H.	Partly closed eyes; in question
D - 9.	BLURT	I.	Moping
Y - 10.	VIRUSES	J.	Squirm
O - 11.	DREAD	K.	Calms down
M - 12.	APPALACHIAN	L.	Pathetic
Q - 13.	COMPLIMENTS	M.	Referring to that area of mountains in the eastern U.S.
B - 14.	ASTONISHED	N.	Respect
P - 15.	AGONIZED	O.	Great fear
I - 16.	SULKING	P.	Tormented over
J - 17.	FIDGET	Q.	To show kindness by a gift
W - 18.	GNARLED	R.	Written agreement
V - 19.	SHRIVELED	S.	Fake
L - 20.	PITIFUL	T.	Looked like
G - 21.	SUMMONED	U.	Lingered
S - 22.	FORGE	V.	Withered
F - 23.	COMMOTION	W.	Twisted
K - 24.	STABILIZES	X.	Disliked; took exception to for some reason
U - 25.	HOVERED	Y.	Infections

Pinballs Vocabulary Matching 4

___ 1. ESTABLISHED   A. Withered
___ 2. STABILIZES   B. Short top that ties behind the neck and across the back
___ 3. AGONIZED   C. Excitement
___ 4. COMPLIMENTS   D. Infections
___ 5. VIRUSES   E. Community where people live and work cooperatively
___ 6. RESENTED   F. Founded
___ 7. RHYTHMIC   G. Great fear
___ 8. JARRED   H. Politely
___ 9. HALTER   I. Specialty shop
___10. DREAD   J. Repulsed
___11. BLURT   K. Casket; box in which to bury dead person
___12. CLENCHED   L. Related by adoption
___13. COMMUNE   M. Needle used under the skin
___14. SHRIVELED   N. Shocked
___15. DISGUSTED   O. Shout
___16. APPENDECTOMY   P. Having a steady motion
___17. VACCINES   Q. With jaws tightly closed
___18. COFFIN   R. Disliked; took exception to for some reason
___19. FORGE   S. Tormented over
___20. COMMOTION   T. To show kindness by a gift
___21. ADOPTIVE   U. Preventative shots
___22. HYPODERMIC   V. Calms down
___23. RESPECTFULLY   W. Fake
___24. BOUTIQUE   X. Bumped
___25. ASTONISHED   Y. Operation to remove appendix

Pinballs Vocabulary Matching 4 Answer Key

F - 1. ESTABLISHED		A. Withered
V - 2. STABILIZES		B. Short top that ties behind the neck and across the back
S - 3. AGONIZED		C. Excitement
T - 4. COMPLIMENTS		D. Infections
D - 5. VIRUSES		E. Community where people live and work cooperatively
R - 6. RESENTED		F. Founded
P - 7. RHYTHMIC		G. Great fear
X - 8. JARRED		H. Politely
B - 9. HALTER		I. Specialty shop
G -10. DREAD		J. Repulsed
O -11. BLURT		K. Casket; box in which to bury dead person
Q -12. CLENCHED		L. Related by adoption
E -13. COMMUNE		M. Needle used under the skin
A -14. SHRIVELED		N. Shocked
J -15. DISGUSTED		O. Shout
Y -16. APPENDECTOMY		P. Having a steady motion
U -17. VACCINES		Q. With jaws tightly closed
K -18. COFFIN		R. Disliked; took exception to for some reason
W -19. FORGE		S. Tormented over
C -20. COMMOTION		T. To show kindness by a gift
L -21. ADOPTIVE		U. Preventative shots
M -22. HYPODERMIC		V. Calms down
H -23. RESPECTFULLY		W. Fake
I -24. BOUTIQUE		X. Bumped
N -25. ASTONISHED		Y. Operation to remove appendix

Pinballs Vocabulary Magic Squares 1

Match the definition with the vocabulary word. Put your answers in the magic squares below. When your answers are correct, all columns and rows will add to the same number.

A. PITIFUL
B. FORGE
C. MINE
D. RESEMBLED
E. RESPECTFULLY
F. ASTONISHED
G. SUSPICION
H. APPENDECTOMY
I. INCISIONS
J. VACCINES
K. COMPLIMENTS
L. ESTABLISHED
M. REFLECTION
N. SUMMONED
O. GNARLED
P. COMMUNE

1. Twisted
2. Preventative shots
3. Operation to remove appendix
4. Pathetic
5. Looked like
6. Politely
7. To show kindness by a gift
8. Called; requested
9. Shocked
10. A quarry or well
11. Likeness; mirror image
12. Founded
13. Cuts
14. Community where people live and work cooperatively
15. Fake
16. Distrust

A=	B=	C=	D=
E=	F=	G=	H=
I=	J=	K=	L=
M=	N=	O=	P=

78
Copyrighted

Pinballs Vocabulary Magic Squares 1 Answer Key

Match the definition with the vocabulary word. Put your answers in the magic squares below. When your answers are correct, all columns and rows will add to the same number.

A. PITIFUL
B. FORGE
C. MINE
D. RESEMBLED
E. RESPECTFULLY
F. ASTONISHED
G. SUSPICION
H. APPENDECTOMY
I. INCISIONS
J. VACCINES
K. COMPLIMENTS
L. ESTABLISHED
M. REFLECTION
N. SUMMONED
O. GNARLED
P. COMMUNE

1. Twisted
2. Preventative shots
3. Operation to remove appendix
4. Pathetic
5. Looked like
6. Politely
7. To show kindness by a gift
8. Called; requested
9. Shocked
10. A quarry or well
11. Likeness; mirror image
12. Founded
13. Cuts
14. Community where people live and work cooperatively
15. Fake
16. Distrust

A=4	B=15	C=10	D=5
E=6	F=9	G=16	H=3
I=13	J=2	K=7	L=12
M=11	N=8	O=1	P=14

Pinballs Vocabulary Magic Squares 2

Match the definition with the vocabulary word. Put your answers in the magic squares below. When your answers are correct, all columns and rows will add to the same number.

A. HYPODERMIC
B. COMMUNE
C. APPEALED
D. INCISIONS
E. MINE
F. SUPERIOR
G. CONCUSSION
H. BLURT
I. RESENTED
J. REFLECTION
K. STABILIZES
L. COMPLIMENTS
M. ADMIRATION
N. COFFIN
O. HALTER
P. BOUTIQUE

1. Short top that ties behind the neck and across the back
2. Cuts
3. Likeness; mirror image
4. A quarry or well
5. Disliked; took exception to for some reason
6. Snobbish; better than others
7. Specialty shop
8. Attracted
9. Shout
10. Calms down
11. Needle used under the skin
12. Casket; box in which to bury dead person
13. Community where people live and work cooperatively
14. Respect
15. Swelling from a blow
16. To show kindness by a gift

A=	B=	C=	D=
E=	F=	G=	H=
I=	J=	K=	L=
M=	N=	O=	P=

Pinballs Vocabulary Magic Squares 2 Answer Key

Match the definition with the vocabulary word. Put your answers in the magic squares below. When your answers are correct, all columns and rows will add to the same number.

A. HYPODERMIC
B. COMMUNE
C. APPEALED
D. INCISIONS
E. MINE
F. SUPERIOR
G. CONCUSSION
H. BLURT
I. RESENTED
J. REFLECTION
K. STABILIZES
L. COMPLIMENTS
M. ADMIRATION
N. COFFIN
O. HALTER
P. BOUTIQUE

1. Short top that ties behind the neck and across the back
2. Cuts
3. Likeness; mirror image
4. A quarry or well
5. Disliked; took exception to for some reason
6. Snobbish; better than others
7. Specialty shop
8. Attracted
9. Shout
10. Calms down
11. Needle used under the skin
12. Casket; box in which to bury dead person
13. Community where people live and work cooperatively
14. Respect
15. Swelling from a blow
16. To show kindness by a gift

A=11	B=13	C=8	D=2
E=4	F=6	G=15	H=9
I=5	J=3	K=10	L=16
M=14	N=12	O=1	P=7

Pinballs Vocabulary Magic Squares 3

Match the definition with the vocabulary word. Put your answers in the magic squares below. When your answers are correct, all columns and rows will add to the same number.

A. BOUTIQUE
B. AGONIZED
C. FIDGET
D. COFFIN
E. SULKING
F. SPIGOT
G. STABILIZES
H. HALTER
I. COMMOTION
J. FORGE
K. SQUINTED
L. CONTRACT
M. APPALACHIAN
N. HYPODERMIC
O. REFLECTION
P. SUSPICION

1. Tormented over
2. Calms down
3. Partly closed eyes; in question
4. Needle used under the skin
5. Referring to that area of mountains in the eastern U.S.
6. Written agreement
7. Short top that ties behind the neck and across the back
8. Specialty shop
9. Distrust
10. Excitement
11. Moping
12. Casket; box in which to bury dead person
13. Squirm
14. Faucet
15. Fake
16. Likeness; mirror image

A=	B=	C=	D=
E=	F=	G=	H=
I=	J=	K=	L=
M=	N=	O=	P=

Pinballs Vocabulary Magic Squares 3 Answer Key

Match the definition with the vocabulary word. Put your answers in the magic squares below. When your answers are correct, all columns and rows will add to the same number.

A. BOUTIQUE
B. AGONIZED
C. FIDGET
D. COFFIN
E. SULKING
F. SPIGOT

G. STABILIZES
H. HALTER
I. COMMOTION
J. FORGE
K. SQUINTED
L. CONTRACT

M. APPALACHIAN
N. HYPODERMIC
O. REFLECTION
P. SUSPICION

1. Tormented over
2. Calms down
3. Partly closed eyes; in question
4. Needle used under the skin
5. Referring to that area of mountains in the eastern U.S.
6. Written agreement
7. Short top that ties behind the neck and across the back
8. Specialty shop
9. Distrust
10. Excitement
11. Moping
12. Casket; box in which to bury dead person
13. Squirm
14. Faucet
15. Fake
16. Likeness; mirror image

A=8	B=1	C=13	D=12
E=11	F=14	G=2	H=7
I=10	J=15	K=3	L=6
M=5	N=4	O=16	P=9

Pinballs Vocabulary Magic Squares 4

Match the definition with the vocabulary word. Put your answers in the magic squares below. When your answers are correct, all columns and rows will add to the same number.

A. GNARLED
B. HALTER
C. CLAMPED
D. SPIGOT
E. INSULT
F. ADMIRATION
G. REFLECTION
H. APPENDECTOMY
I. AGONIZED
J. UNCOMPLIMENTARY
K. DISGUSTED
L. CONTRACT
M. HUNCHED
N. JARRED
O. COFFIN
P. CLENCHED

1. Respect
2. Tormented over
3. Casket; box in which to bury dead person
4. Faucet
5. Bent
6. Short top that ties behind the neck and across the back
7. Operation to remove appendix
8. Repulsed
9. Tightly closed
10. With jaws tightly closed
11. Negative
12. Offend
13. Written agreement
14. Likeness; mirror image
15. Twisted
16. Bumped

A=	B=	C=	D=
E=	F=	G=	H=
I=	J=	K=	L=
M=	N=	O=	P=

Pinballs Vocabulary Magic Squares 4 Answer Key

Match the definition with the vocabulary word. Put your answers in the magic squares below. When your answers are correct, all columns and rows will add to the same number.

A. GNARLED
B. HALTER
C. CLAMPED
D. SPIGOT
E. INSULT
F. ADMIRATION
G. REFLECTION
H. APPENDECTOMY
I. AGONIZED
J. UNCOMPLIMENTARY
K. DISGUSTED
L. CONTRACT
M. HUNCHED
N. JARRED
O. COFFIN
P. CLENCHED

1. Respect
2. Tormented over
3. Casket; box in which to bury dead person
4. Faucet
5. Bent
6. Short top that ties behind the neck and across the back
7. Operation to remove appendix
8. Repulsed
9. Tightly closed
10. With jaws tightly closed
11. Negative
12. Offend
13. Written agreement
14. Likeness; mirror image
15. Twisted
16. Bumped

A=15	B=6	C=9	D=4
E=12	F=1	G=14	H=7
I=2	J=11	K=8	L=13
M=5	N=16	O=3	P=10

Pinballs Vocabulary Word Search 1

```
C V P G N A R L E D D Y P H J G P B S W
L M I W W N E N U M M O C D A E R D U N
A M T R X P G Q L O D Z B D R S L E P T
M K I K U N K T T Q H Z M F R D M L E C
P T F W I S G C C N O I T C E L F E R T
E B U K Y V E M K O R B H L D Z H V I F
D D L R H D S S M A M H B U K J F I O X
L U V U N M C D T F P M Y R N C X R R L
S S T E R H C I I X E P O T M C Y H G X
Z P P A S T O N I S H E D T H S H S K X
W P I G Z N M V E S G X F K I M Z E F M
A G X G C J P R E Q G U M T A O I T D C
V E G R O F L N S R K H S M P W N C A M
B S B O U T I Q U E E V I T P O D A P W
S W M B S C M D M R Q D F V E P E R P W
H U H F C G E K G K R K B D A D T T A P
H B M A B S N J D E H C N E L C N N L L
F N V M V L T I S B T X F Z E D I O A M
G Z Q L O X S E N L D Q J I D T U C C W
C O F F I N N O I S S U C N O C Q P H M
K H X W J T E Z V S U C K O X F S X I F
N M M M E K D D M L C L C G X M V N A N
X L P D H A L T E R P M T A V Q E Z N T
```

A quarry or well (4)
Attracted (8)
Bent (7)
Bumped (6)
Called; requested (8)
Casket; box in which to bury dead person (6)
Community where people live and work cooperatively (7)
Disliked; took exception to for some reason (8)
Excitement (9)
Fake (5)
Faucet (6)
Great fear (5)
Having a steady motion (8)
Infections (7)
Likeness; mirror image (10)
Lingered (7)
Looked like (9)
Moping (7)
Offend (6)
Operation to remove appendix (12)
Partly closed eyes; in question (8)

Pathetic (7)
Preventative shots (8)
Referring to that area of mountains in the eastern U.S. (11)
Related by adoption (8)
Repulsed (9)
Respect (10)
Shocked (10)
Short top that ties behind the neck and across the back (6)
Shout (5)
Snobbish; better than others (8)
Specialty shop (8)
Squirm (6)
Swelling from a blow (10)
Tightly closed (7)
To show kindness by a gift (11)
Tormented over (8)
Twisted (7)
With jaws tightly closed (8)
Withered (9)
Written agreement (8)

Pinballs Vocabulary Word Search 1 Answer Key

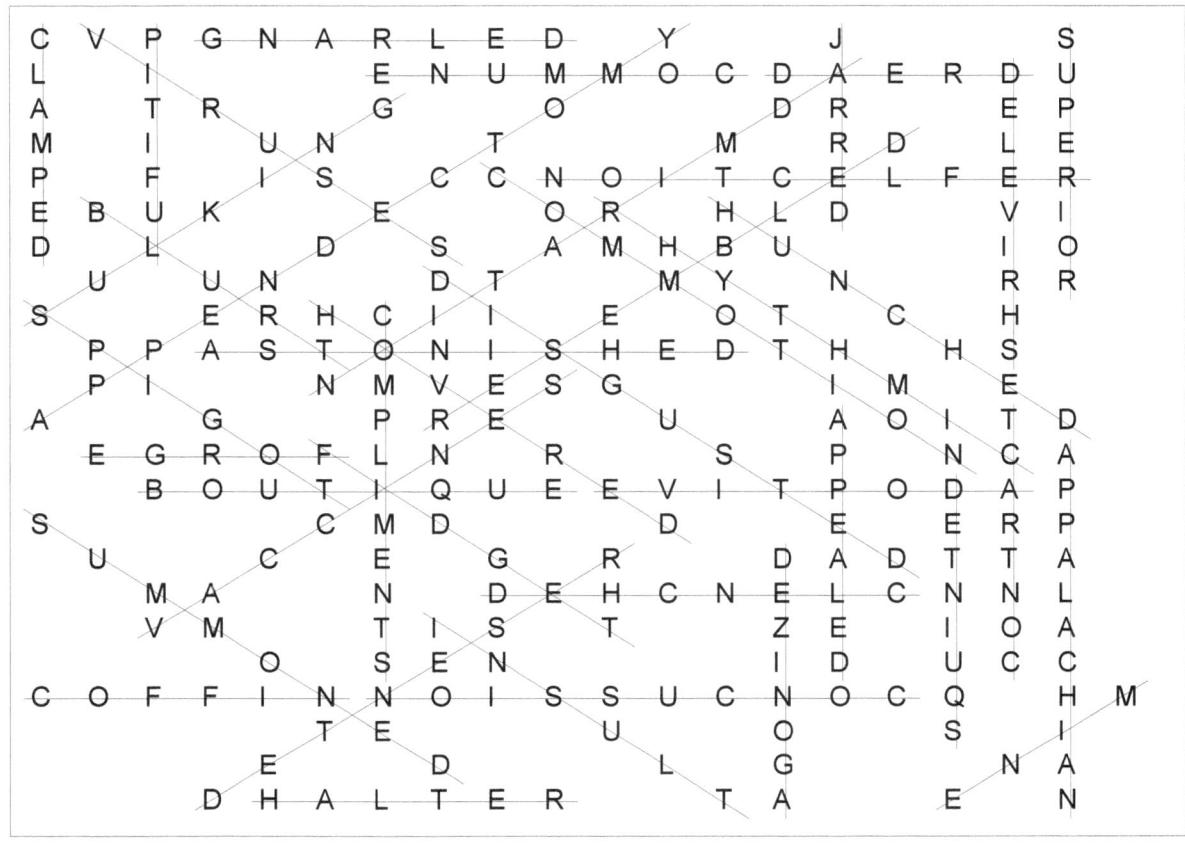

A quarry or well (4)
Attracted (8)
Bent (7)
Bumped (6)
Called; requested (8)
Casket; box in which to bury dead person (6)
Community where people live and work cooperatively (7)
Disliked; took exception to for some reason (8)
Excitement (9)
Fake (5)
Faucet (6)
Great fear (5)
Having a steady motion (8)
Infections (7)
Likeness; mirror image (10)
Lingered (7)
Looked like (9)
Moping (7)
Offend (6)
Operation to remove appendix (12)
Partly closed eyes; in question (8)

Pathetic (7)
Preventative shots (8)
Referring to that area of mountains in the eastern U.S. (11)
Related by adoption (8)
Repulsed (9)
Respect (10)
Shocked (10)
Short top that ties behind the neck and across the back (6)
Shout (5)
Snobbish; better than others (8)
Specialty shop (8)
Squirm (6)
Swelling from a blow (10)
Tightly closed (7)
To show kindness by a gift (11)
Tormented over (8)
Twisted (7)
With jaws tightly closed (8)
Withered (9)
Written agreement (8)

Pinballs Vocabulary Word Search 2

```
A P P A L A C H I A N O I T O M M O C Z
C L C J X D A O O M P H S D P D Z B O J
L N K N A L C X F V L P U P R D B L M R
E L P E T R N L Z F E T E N I Q P U M S
N F R E P S R L A J I R J A C G M R U Y
C D R X I T U E N M W N E P L H O T N T
H L E Y T D Q M D H P N T D C E E T E Z
E G S R I E D R M T X E E C O R D D G X
D N E A F C A J X O S T D I N H W I F Y
Z I M T U J K R P T N N K M C Y P S T N
L K B N L T Y V N I K E Q R U T T G G T
K L L E Y H R E U E J V D E S H L U Q A
G U E M T W M Q N N S I W D S M B S S R
Y S D I X I S G L O Z T J O I L T I B
F B U L L N Y J Z I J P L P O C O E N N
V R A P P E N D E C T O M Y N N E D S L
J A M M E V G P F I M D K H I U E E U H
B O C O T R W Z H P I A F S Q Z W L L Y
C I N C I S I O N S N J H I I F E R T K
R K Q N I G V O M U E E T N D G P A R Y
M R F U D N F C R S D U O Z R G R N N M
R E S E N T E D C Q O G Q O R L E G S Y
D V I R U S E S G B A N F Z Q W M T L Q
```

A quarry or well (4)
Attracted (8)
Bent (7)
Bumped (6)
Called; requested (8)
Casket; box in which to bury dead person (6)
Community where people live and work cooperatively (7)
Cuts (9)
Disliked; took exception to for some reason (8)
Distrust (9)
Excitement (9)
Fake (5)
Faucet (6)
Great fear (5)
Having a steady motion (8)
Infections (7)
Lingered (7)
Looked like (9)
Moping (7)
Needle used under the skin (10)
Negative (15)

Offend (6)
Operation to remove appendix (12)
Partly closed eyes; in question (8)
Pathetic (7)
Preventative shots (8)
Referring to that area of mountains in the eastern U.S. (11)
Related by adoption (8)
Repulsed (9)
Shocked (10)
Short top that ties behind the neck and across the back (6)
Shout (5)
Sincerely (9)
Snobbish; better than others (8)
Specialty shop (8)
Squirm (6)
Swelling from a blow (10)
Tightly closed (7)
To show kindness by a gift (11)
Tormented over (8)
Twisted (7)
With jaws tightly closed (8)

Pinballs Vocabulary Word Search 2 Answer Key

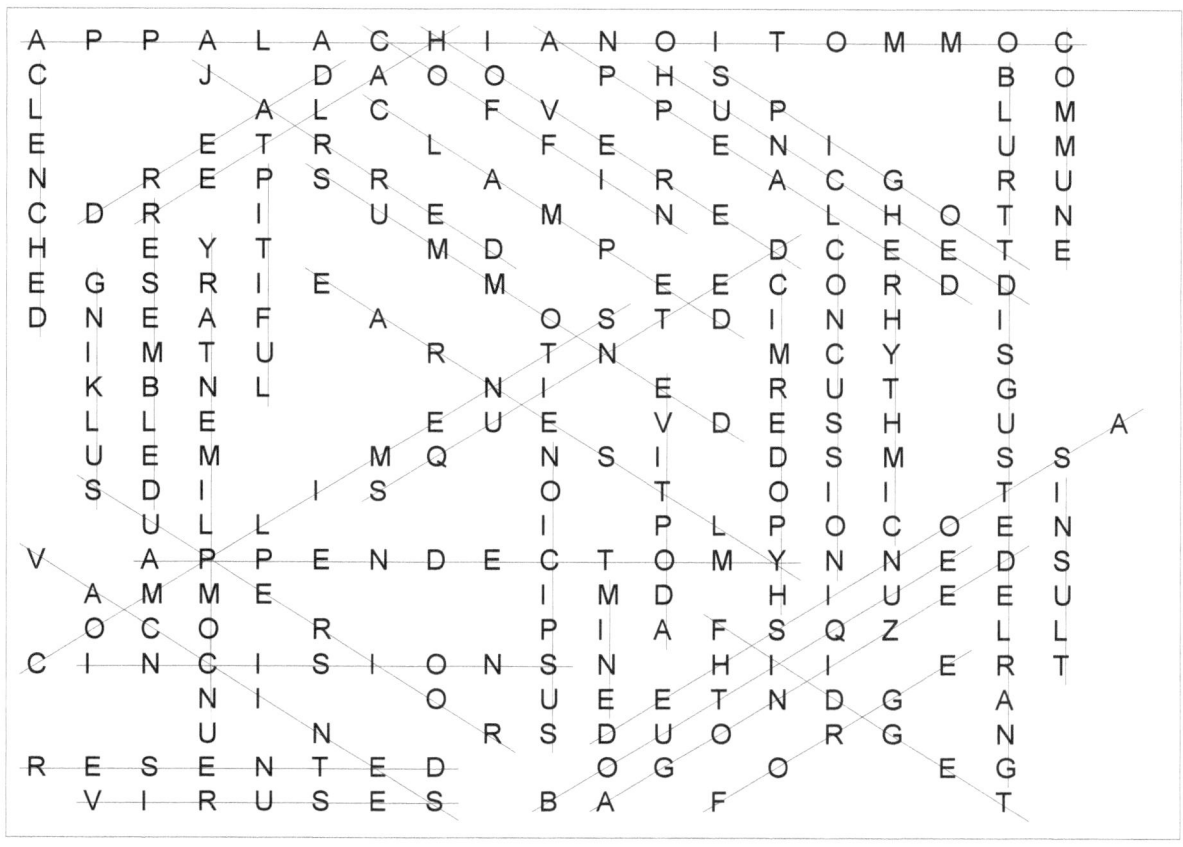

A quarry or well (4)
Attracted (8)
Bent (7)
Bumped (6)
Called; requested (8)
Casket; box in which to bury dead person (6)
Community where people live and work cooperatively (7)
Cuts (9)
Disliked; took exception to for some reason (8)
Distrust (9)
Excitement (9)
Fake (5)
Faucet (6)
Great fear (5)
Having a steady motion (8)
Infections (7)
Lingered (7)
Looked like (9)
Moping (7)
Needle used under the skin (10)
Negative (15)
Offend (6)
Operation to remove appendix (12)
Partly closed eyes; in question (8)
Pathetic (7)
Preventative shots (8)
Referring to that area of mountains in the eastern U.S. (11)
Related by adoption (8)
Repulsed (9)
Shocked (10)
Short top that ties behind the neck and across the back (6)
Shout (5)
Sincerely (9)
Snobbish; better than others (8)
Specialty shop (8)
Squirm (6)
Swelling from a blow (10)
Tightly closed (7)
To show kindness by a gift (11)
Tormented over (8)
Twisted (7)
With jaws tightly closed (8)

Pinballs Vocabulary Word Search 3

```
W H L B A D O P T I V E D E Z K N B A D
D Y B C S G Q V J V Q E K A D C D Z P G
E V W I T Z T H Y J T R D R V W I P P M
H T Y M O K M M N N E D Y N T F S N E V
S Q D R N F H N I S W V M E X K G H N S
I S T E I B V U E F H W C S S X U A D N
L U B D S P Q N F J N P P T E M S L E Y
B P G O H S T P Q O W N D L S I T C Q N
A E N P E E T T I R B S S Y U N E E T N
T R A Y D E H C N U H O V E R E D R O M
S I R H D Q I I O R V Y U Z I D G I M L
E O L A G P F T I N A F T T V G T Z Y M
B R E V S F R V T M C P O H I O H N C X
P R D U O U E P A R C U F R M Q A H L P
D E S C L L S I R T I F S M G I U L A Q
C S U B E I E T I W N Q O S H E C E M Y
O P L D A N M I M B E C D C I C L I P D
N E K B P S B F D F S E A D Z O E N E G
T C I X P U L U A T Z L E B F M N C D Z
R T N F E L E L S I A N J D R M C I L Q
A F G T A T D T N P O S E P N U H S G L
C U B X L D D O P M I R X C L N E I P H
T L F T E T G A M N R G T X Z E D O R X
D L P R D A D U Q A D G O P T P X N H C
V Y W Q Y P S G J P Z F K T F N G S G K
```

ADMIRATION COMMOTION HOVERED SHRIVELED

ADOPTIVE COMMUNE HUNCHED SPIGOT

AGONIZED CONCUSSION HYPODERMIC SQUINTED

APPALACHIAN CONTRACT INCISIONS SULKING

APPEALED DISGUSTED INSULT SUMMONED

APPENDECTOMY DREAD JARRED SUPERIOR

ASTONISHED EARNESTLY MINE SUSPICION

BLURT ESTABLISHED PITIFUL VACCINES

BOUTIQUE FIDGET RESEMBLED VIRUSES

CLAMPED FORGE RESENTED

CLENCHED GNARLED RESPECTFULLY

COFFIN HALTER RHYTHMIC

Pinballs Vocabulary Word Search 3 Answer Key

[Word search grid]

ADMIRATION	COMMOTION	HOVERED	SHRIVELED
ADOPTIVE	COMMUNE	HUNCHED	SPIGOT
AGONIZED	CONCUSSION	HYPODERMIC	SQUINTED
APPALACHIAN	CONTRACT	INCISIONS	SULKING
APPEALED	DISGUSTED	INSULT	SUMMONED
APPENDECTOMY	DREAD	JARRED	SUPERIOR
ASTONISHED	EARNESTLY	MINE	SUSPICION
BLURT	ESTABLISHED	PITIFUL	VACCINES
BOUTIQUE	FIDGET	RESEMBLED	VIRUSES
CLAMPED	FORGE	RESENTED	
CLENCHED	GNARLED	RESPECTFULLY	
COFFIN	HALTER	RHYTHMIC	

Pinballs Vocabulary Word Search 4

```
C O M M O T I O N A G O N I Z E D E M T
O Q C S R R Y T P I T I F U L E C A U W
M P L R Q M P P N Y Y W E W S S H R N G
M P A Z R U E O D D W X U F E T T N C G
U G M B G A I E S B G P Q N Z A N E O Z
N Z P J L C T N Q U R Y I S K B Z S M R
E C E E I S B T T Z M C T Z B L I T P Y
X N D P U H P T W E C M U P T N L L P P
X D S G K J R M X A D T O W L S S Y I B
M U S V P U S I V F C C B N C H U K M F
S I H F L D G N D A I Z X Y E E L T E Z
D E L B M E S E R G P D R A D T G N G M
Z P A K N G R T J R E E T S E N O T A M
A F D Q M R N S F L B R C E V H I R A T
W P O B A O S V E H W E D Q T S Y E R R
L T P J C F B V Y Q J V X T S I N S Y K
N J T E Q T I P P S T O I U F N O E I D
S N I X N R O D D N K H C R P O I N N W
Q M V Y H D D E L R A N G O U T T C C R
L D E S E N E H R G O F N I S S C E I R
B J L R I N H C E C Q S I R P A E D S C
Z J M F L T C N T F D L K E I R L S I Z
T I F X C S N E L O K K L P G L F X O P
C O F K S Y U L A J M N U U O X E Z N Y
C W T G S R H C H T Q Y S S T R R Z S C
```

ADOPTIVE	DREAD	REFLECTION
AGONIZED	EARNESTLY	RESEMBLED
APPEALED	ESTABLISHED	RESENTED
APPENDECTOMY	FIDGET	SHRIVELED
ASTONISHED	FORGE	SPIGOT
BLURT	GNARLED	SQUINTED
BOUTIQUE	HALTER	SULKING
CLAMPED	HOVERED	SUMMONED
CLENCHED	HUNCHED	SUPERIOR
COFFIN	HYPODERMIC	SUSPICION
COMMOTION	INCISIONS	UNCOMPLIMENTARY
COMMUNE	INSULT	VACCINES
CONCUSSION	JARRED	VIRUSES
CONTRACT	MINE	
DISGUSTED	PITIFUL	

Pinballs Vocabulary Word Search 4 Answer Key

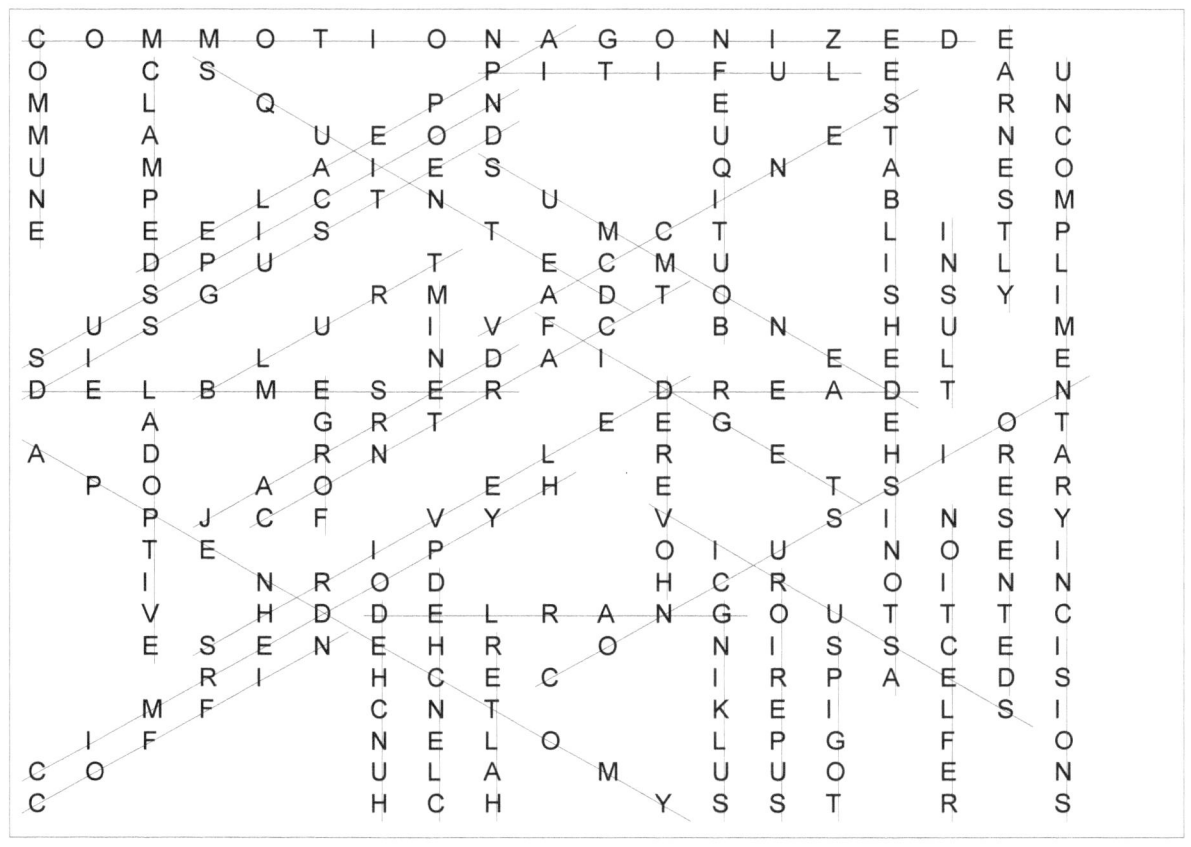

ADOPTIVE	DREAD	REFLECTION
AGONIZED	EARNESTLY	RESEMBLED
APPEALED	ESTABLISHED	RESENTED
APPENDECTOMY	FIDGET	SHRIVELED
ASTONISHED	FORGE	SPIGOT
BLURT	GNARLED	SQUINTED
BOUTIQUE	HALTER	SULKING
CLAMPED	HOVERED	SUMMONED
CLENCHED	HUNCHED	SUPERIOR
COFFIN	HYPODERMIC	SUSPICION
COMMOTION	INCISIONS	UNCOMPLIMENTARY
COMMUNE	INSULT	VACCINES
CONCUSSION	JARRED	VIRUSES
CONTRACT	MINE	
DISGUSTED	PITIFUL	

Pinballs Vocabulary Crossword 1

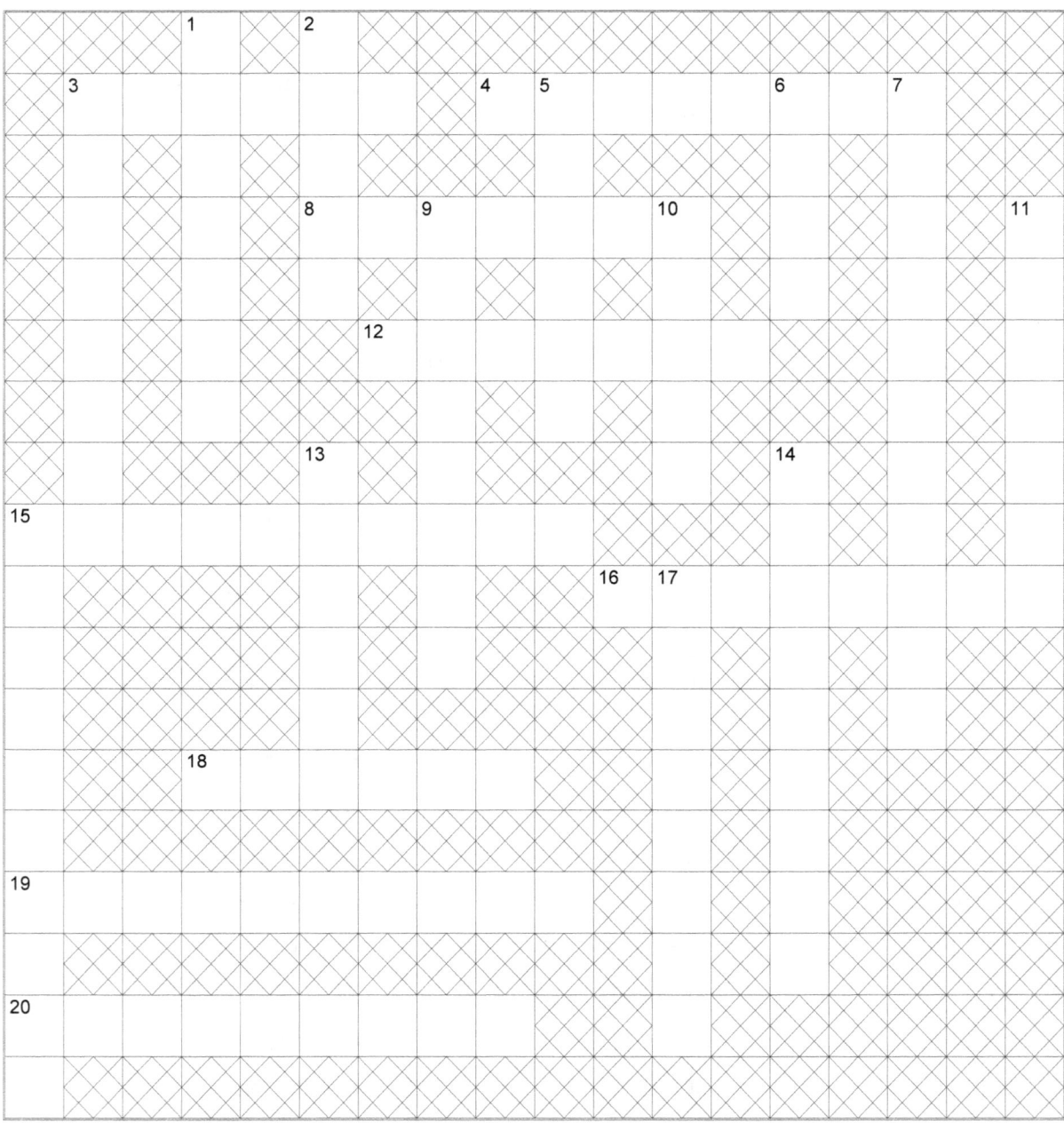

Across
3. Faucet
4. Having a steady motion
8. Twisted
12. Lingered
15. Respect
16. Preventative shots
18. Squirm
19. Calms down
20. Sincerely

Down
1. Pathetic
2. Fake
3. Called; requested
5. Short top that ties behind the neck and across the back
6. A quarry or well
7. To show kindness by a gift
9. Related by adoption
10. Great fear
11. Infections
13. Bumped
14. Cuts
15. Shocked
17. Tormented over

Pinballs Vocabulary Crossword 1 Answer Key

		1		2							
		P		F							
	3					4	5		6	7	
	S	P	I	G	O	T	R	H	Y	T	H	M	I	C
	U	T		R			A			I		O		
	M	I		8 G	9 N	A	R	L	10 E	D		N	M	11 V
	M	F		E	D		T		R			E	P	I
	O	U			12 H	O	V	E	R	E	D		L	R
	N	L					P		R			A	I	U
	E			13 J		T			D		14 I		M	S
15 A	D	M	I	R	A	T	I	O	N			N	E	E
S				R		V			16 V	17 A	C	C	I	N	E	S
T				R		E			G		I		T	
O				E					O		S		S	
N			18 F	I	D	G	E	T		N		I		
I										I		O		
19 S	T	A	B	I	L	I	Z	E	S		Z		N	
H											E		S	
20 E	A	R	N	E	S	T	L	Y			D			
D														

Across
 3. Faucet
 4. Having a steady motion
 8. Twisted
 12. Lingered
 15. Respect
 16. Preventative shots
 18. Squirm
 19. Calms down
 20. Sincerely

Down
 1. Pathetic
 2. Fake
 3. Called; requested
 5. Short top that ties behind the neck and across the back
 6. A quarry or well
 7. To show kindness by a gift
 9. Related by adoption
 10. Great fear
 11. Infections
 13. Bumped
 14. Cuts
 15. Shocked
 17. Tormented over

Pinballs Vocabulary Crossword 2

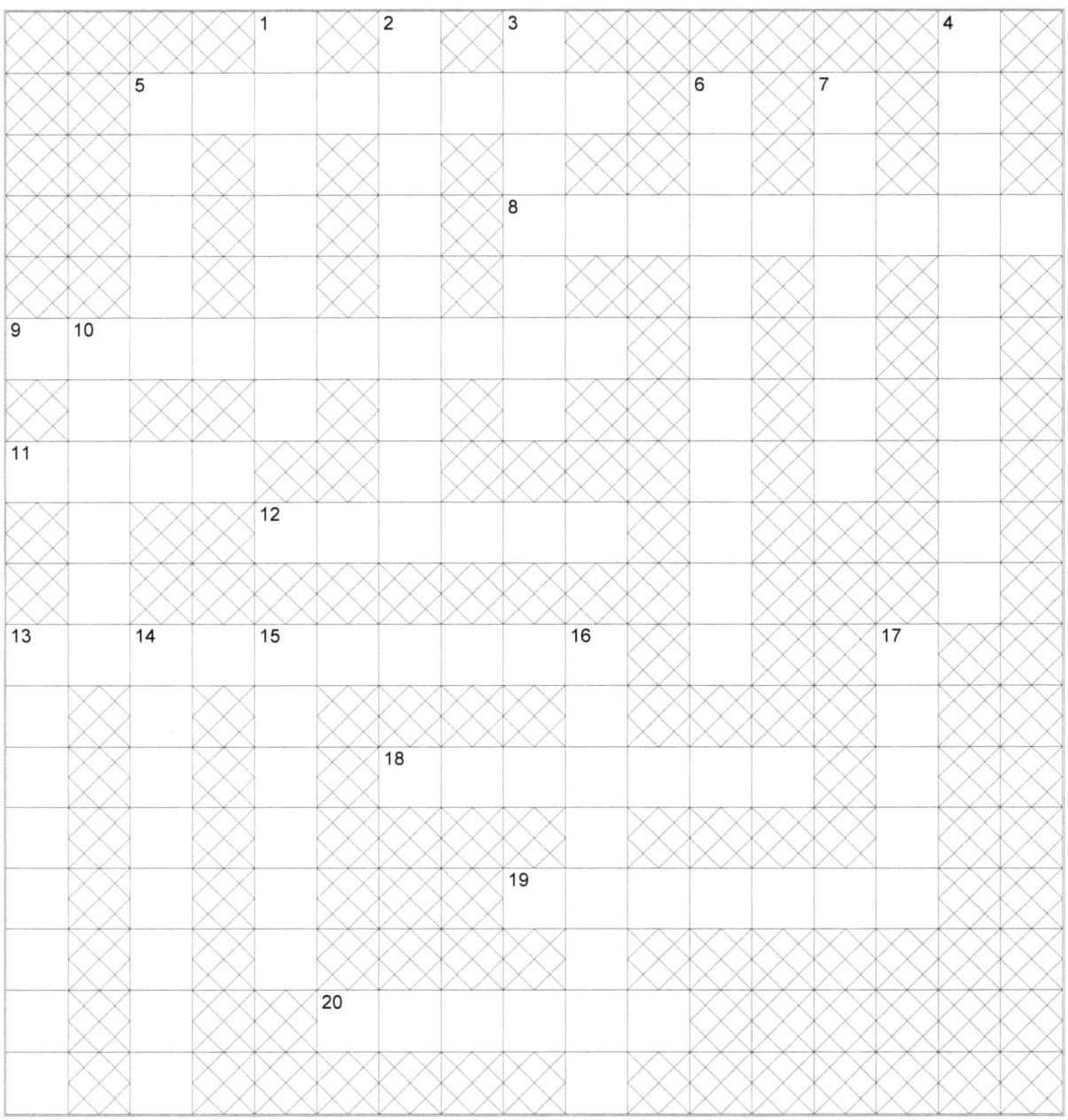

Across
5. Specialty shop
8. Excitement
9. Shocked
11. A quarry or well
12. Squirm
13. Calms down
18. Infections
19. Twisted
20. Short top that ties behind the neck and across the back

Down
1. Moping
2. Repulsed
3. Bent
4. Needle used under the skin
5. Shout
6. Respect
7. Pathetic
10. Faucet
13. Called; requested
14. Tormented over
15. Offend
16. Partly closed eyes; in question
17. Great fear

Pinballs Vocabulary Crossword 2 Answer Key

			S		D		H					H	
		B	O	U	T	I	Q	U	E	A		P	Y
		L		L		S		N		D		I	P
		U		K		G		C	O	M	M	O	T	I	O	N
		R		I		U		H		I		I	D
A	S	T	O	N	I	S	H	E	D	R		F	E
	P			G		T		D		A		U	R
M	I	N	E			E				T		L	M
	G			F	I	D	G	E	T	I			I
	O									O			C
S	T	A	B	I	L	I	Z	E	S	N		D	
U		G		N				Q				R	
M		O		S		V	I	R	U	S	E	S	
M		N		U		I		I				A	
O		I		L		G	N	A	R	L	E	D	
N		Z		T		N		T					
E		E		H	A	L	T	E	R				
D		D						D					

Across
- 5. Specialty shop
- 8. Excitement
- 9. Shocked
- 11. A quarry or well
- 12. Squirm
- 13. Calms down
- 18. Infections
- 19. Twisted
- 20. Short top that ties behind the neck and across the back

Down
- 1. Moping
- 2. Repulsed
- 3. Bent
- 4. Needle used under the skin
- 5. Shout
- 6. Respect
- 7. Pathetic
- 10. Faucet
- 13. Called; requested
- 14. Tormented over
- 15. Offend
- 16. Partly closed eyes; in question
- 17. Great fear

Pinballs Vocabulary Crossword 3

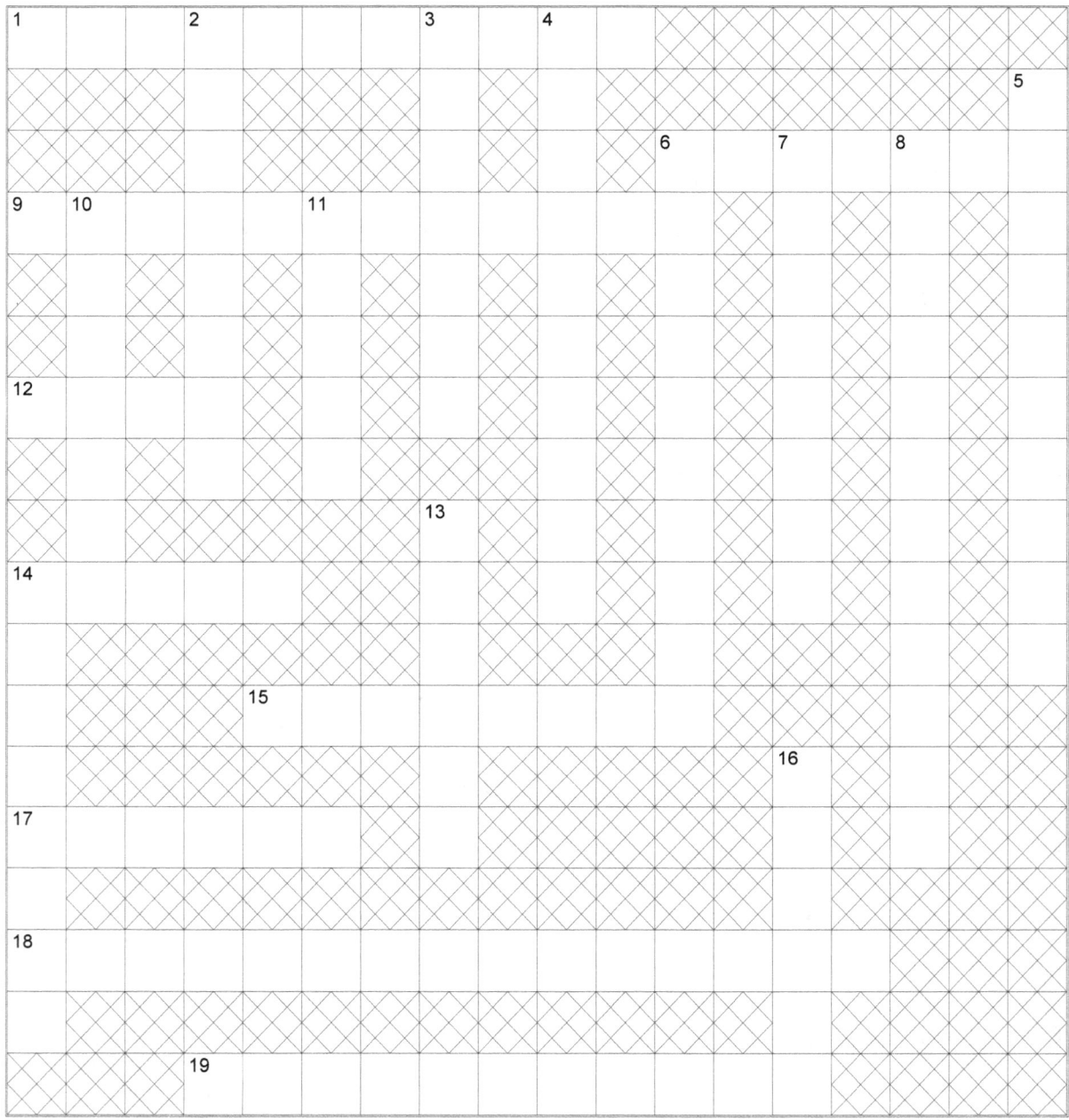

Across
1. Referring to that area of mountains in the eastern U.S.
6. Lingered
9. Operation to remove appendix
12. A quarry or well
14. Shout
15. Having a steady motion
17. Offend
18. Negative
19. Founded

Down
2. Attracted
3. Bent
4. Shocked
5. Respect
6. Needle used under the skin
7. Preventative shots
8. Politely
10. Pathetic
11. Great fear
13. Short top that ties behind the neck and across the back
14. Specialty shop
16. Bumped

Pinballs Vocabulary Crossword 3 Answer Key

	1 A	2 P	P	A	L	A	C	3 H	I	4 A	N			
			P					U		S				5 A
			P					N		T		6 H	7 O	8 V	E	R	E	D
9 A	10 P	P	E	N	11 D	E	C	T	O	M	Y		A		E		M
	I		A		R			H		N		P		C		S		I
	T		L		E			E		I		O		C		P		R
12 M	I	N	E		A			D		S		D		I		E		A
	F		D		D			H		E		N		C		T
	U						13 H	E		R		E		T		I
14 B	L	U	R	T			A		D			M		S		F		O
O							L					I				U		N
U			15 R	H	Y	T	H	M	I	C						L
T							E							16 J		L
17 I	N	S	U	L	T		R							A		Y
Q														R
18 U	N	C	O	M	P	L	I	M	E	N	T	A	R	Y
E														E
			19 E	S	T	A	B	L	I	S	H	E	D

Across
1. Referring to that area of mountains in the eastern U.S.
6. Lingered
9. Operation to remove appendix
12. A quarry or well
14. Shout
15. Having a steady motion
17. Offend
18. Negative
19. Founded

Down
2. Attracted
3. Bent
4. Shocked
5. Respect
6. Needle used under the skin
7. Preventative shots
8. Politely
10. Pathetic
11. Great fear
13. Short top that ties behind the neck and across the back
14. Specialty shop
16. Bumped

Pinballs Vocabulary Crossword 4

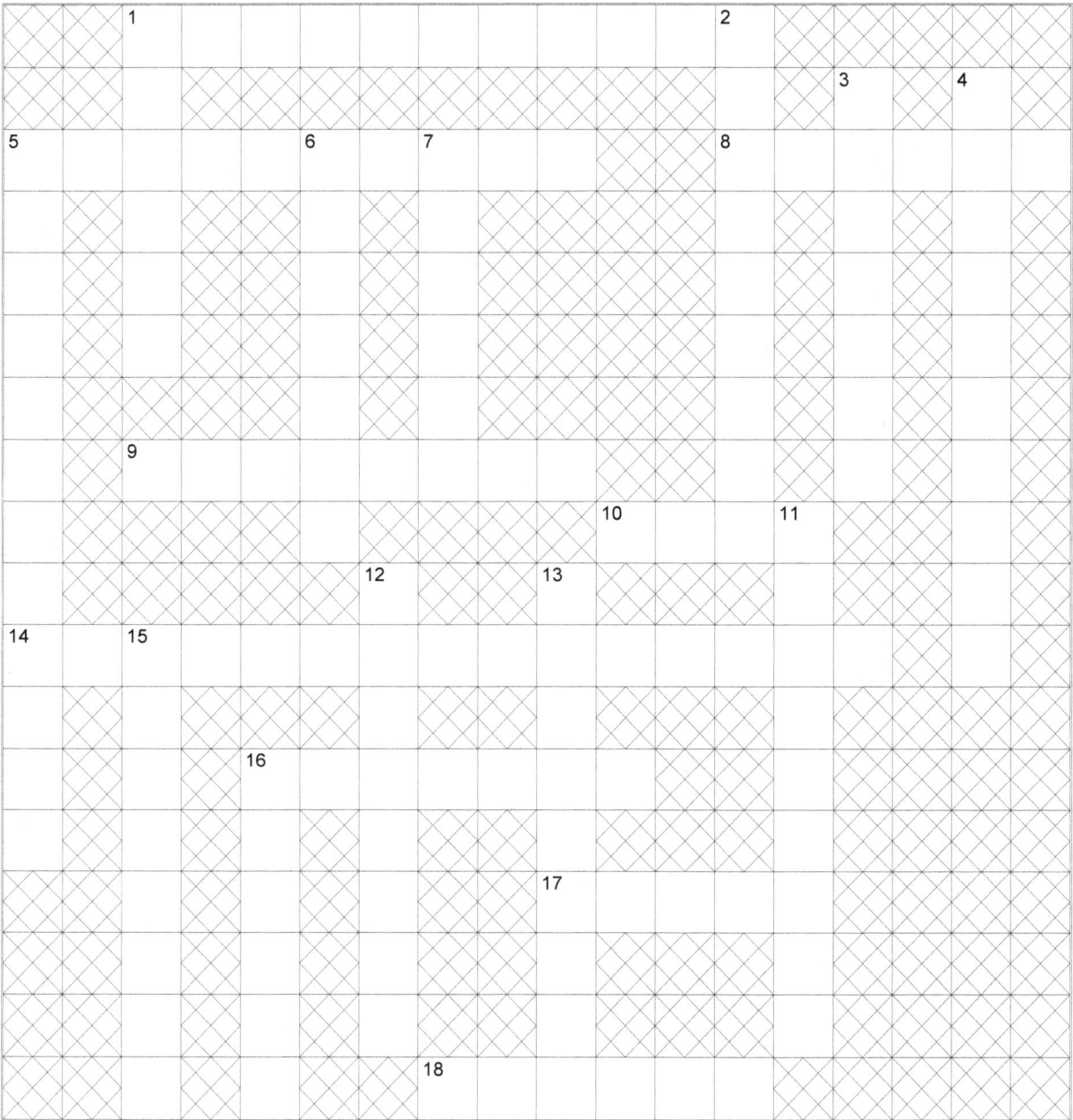

Across
1. To show kindness by a gift
5. Likeness; mirror image
8. Faucet
9. Disliked; took exception to for some reason
10. A quarry or well
14. Negative
16. Bent
17. Shout
18. Squirm

Down
1. Casket; box in which to bury dead person
2. Distrust
3. Pathetic
4. Swelling from a blow
5. Politely
6. Tightly closed
7. Offend
11. Sincerely
12. With jaws tightly closed
13. Looked like
15. Written agreement
16. Short top that ties behind the neck and across the back

Pinballs Vocabulary Crossword 4 Answer Key

	1 C	O	M	P	L	I	M	E	N	T	S 2			
	O										U	P 3	C 4	
R 5	E	F 6	L	E	C 6	T	I 7	O	N		S 8	P	I	G	O	T
E		F			L		N				P		T		N
S		I			A		S				I		I		C
P		N			M		U				C		F		U
E					P		L				I		U		S
C	R 9	E	S	E	N	T	E	D			O		L		S
T				D					M 10	I	N	E 11		I
F					C 12		R 13				A		O
U 14	N	C 15	O	M	P	L	I	M	E	N	T	A	R	Y		N
L		O			E		S				N	
L		N	H 16	U	N	C	H	E	D		E	
Y		T	A		C		M				S	
		R	L		H		B 17	L	U	R	T	
		A	T		E		L			L	
		C	E		D		E			Y	
		T	R		F 18	I	D	G	E	T	

Across
1. To show kindness by a gift
5. Likeness; mirror image
8. Faucet
9. Disliked; took exception to for some reason
10. A quarry or well
14. Negative
16. Bent
17. Shout
18. Squirm

Down
1. Casket; box in which to bury dead person
2. Distrust
3. Pathetic
4. Swelling from a blow
5. Politely
6. Tightly closed
7. Offend
11. Sincerely
12. With jaws tightly closed
13. Looked like
15. Written agreement
16. Short top that ties behind the neck and across the back

Pinballs Vocabulary Juggle Letters 1

1. TNRCOCAT = 1. _____
   Written agreement

2. PTFLULYRCEES = 2. _____
   Politely

3. LINSUKG = 3. _____
   Moping

4. CONUAEIYRTLPMMN = 4. _____
   Negative

5. ZIISBAELTS = 5. _____
   Calms down

6. RDREJA = 6. _____
   Bumped

7. HITMYCHR = 7. _____
   Having a steady motion

8. IESRPRUO = 8. _____
   Snobbish; better than others

9. EGFOR = 9. _____
   Fake

10. DNAISHTEOS = 10. _____
    Shocked

11. HDENCUH = 11. _____
    Bent

12. SINSCONII = 12. _____
    Cuts

13. LRDMEEESB = 13. _____
    Looked like

14. TEEESDRN = 14. _____
    Disliked; took exception to for some reason

15. ENQDTUSI = 15. _____
    Partly closed eyes; in question

Pinballs Vocabulary Juggle Letters 1 Answer Key

1. TNRCOCAT = 1. CONTRACT
Written agreement

2. PTFLULYRCEES = 2. RESPECTFULLY
Politely

3. LINSUKG = 3. SULKING
Moping

4. CONUAEIYRTLPMMN = 4. UNCOMPLIMENTARY
Negative

5. ZIISBAELTS = 5. STABILIZES
Calms down

6. RDREJA = 6. JARRED
Bumped

7. HITMYCHR = 7. RHYTHMIC
Having a steady motion

8. IESRPRUO = 8. SUPERIOR
Snobbish; better than others

9. EGFOR = 9. FORGE
Fake

10. DNAISHTEOS =10. ASTONISHED
Shocked

11. HDENCUH =11. HUNCHED
Bent

12. SINSCONII =12. INCISIONS
Cuts

13. LRDMEEESB =13. RESEMBLED
Looked like

14. TEEESDRN =14. RESENTED
Disliked; took exception to for some reason

15. ENQDTUSI =15. SQUINTED
Partly closed eyes; in question

Pinballs Vocabulary Juggle Letters 2

1. BESLDRMEE = 1. _____
   Looked like

2. MOSDUEMN = 2. _____
   Called; requested

3. COCRATTN = 3. _____
   Written agreement

4. LBRUT = 4. _____
   Shout

5. EEDNHCLC = 5. _____
   With jaws tightly closed

6. IVHDRELSE = 6. _____
   Withered

7. TSBSIEAIZL = 7. _____
   Calms down

8. FUIIPTL = 8. _____
   Pathetic

9. RAENGDL = 9. _____
   Twisted

10. PAIALACHAPN =10. _____
    Referring to that area of mountains in the eastern U.S.

11. MUETNYRNPLCIOAM =11. _____
    Negative

12. IRTODMIANA =12. _____
    Respect

13. ONMEMUC =13. _____
    Community where people live and work cooperatively

14. YRLEULPTECSF =14. _____
    Politely

15. ISOTGP =15. _____
    Faucet

Pinballs Vocabulary Juggle Letters 2 Answer Key

1. BESLDRMEE = 1. RESEMBLED
   Looked like

2. MOSDUEMN = 2. SUMMONED
   Called; requested

3. COCRATTN = 3. CONTRACT
   Written agreement

4. LBRUT = 4. BLURT
   Shout

5. EEDNHCLC = 5. CLENCHED
   With jaws tightly closed

6. IVHDRELSE = 6. SHRIVELED
   Withered

7. TSBSIEAIZL = 7. STABILIZES
   Calms down

8. FUIIPTL = 8. PITIFUL
   Pathetic

9. RAENGDL = 9. GNARLED
   Twisted

10. PAIALACHAPN =10. APPALACHIAN
    Referring to that area of mountains in the eastern U.S.

11. MUETNYRNPLCIOAM =11. UNCOMPLIMENTARY
    Negative

12. IRTODMIANA =12. ADMIRATION
    Respect

13. ONMEMUC =13. COMMUNE
    Community where people live and work cooperatively

14. YRLEULPTECSF =14. RESPECTFULLY
    Politely

15. ISOTGP =15. SPIGOT
    Faucet

Pinballs Vocabulary Juggle Letters 3

1. IRESUORP = 1. _____
   Snobbish; better than others

2. EPYLRLUCESFT = 2. _____
   Politely

3. DREJRA = 3. _____
   Bumped

4. OOCNOTIMM = 4. _____
   Excitement

5. NFFICO = 5. _____
   Casket; box in which to bury dead person

6. PALANCPAHAI = 6. _____
   Referring to that area of mountains in the eastern U.S.

7. DRVESILEH = 7. _____
   Withered

8. INSSNCIOI = 8. _____
   Cuts

9. LRNITEOCEF = 9. _____
   Likeness; mirror image

10. OGPITS =10. _____
    Faucet

11. QIEDNTUS =11. _____
    Partly closed eyes; in question

12. DEHREOV =12. _____
    Lingered

13. LTRUB =13. _____
    Shout

14. UNSNOICCSO =14. _____
    Swelling from a blow

15. EDARD =15. _____
    Great fear

Pinballs Vocabulary Juggle Letters 3 Answer Key

1. IRESUORP = 1. SUPERIOR
   Snobbish; better than others

2. EPYLRLUCESFT = 2. RESPECTFULLY
   Politely

3. DREJRA = 3. JARRED
   Bumped

4. OOCNOTIMM = 4. COMMOTION
   Excitement

5. NFFICO = 5. COFFIN
   Casket; box in which to bury dead person

6. PALANCPAHAI = 6. APPALACHIAN
   Referring to that area of mountains in the eastern U.S.

7. DRVESILEH = 7. SHRIVELED
   Withered

8. INSSNCIOI = 8. INCISIONS
   Cuts

9. LRNITEOCEF = 9. REFLECTION
   Likeness; mirror image

10. OGPITS =10. SPIGOT
    Faucet

11. QIEDNTUS =11. SQUINTED
    Partly closed eyes; in question

12. DEHREOV =12. HOVERED
    Lingered

13. LTRUB =13. BLURT
    Shout

14. UNSNOICCSO =14. CONCUSSION
    Swelling from a blow

15. EDARD =15. DREAD
    Great fear

Pinballs Vocabulary Juggle Letters 4

1. MICLTMNEOSP = 1. _____
   To show kindness by a gift

2. VRDHEOE = 2. _____
   Lingered

3. EARDRJ = 3. _____
   Bumped

4. ISSINNCOI = 4. _____
   Cuts

5. PADLEEAP = 5. _____
   Attracted

6. OMCUENM = 6. _____
   Community where people live and work cooperatively

7. GDLENAR = 7. _____
   Twisted

8. SCINNOOCSU = 8. _____
   Swelling from a blow

9. TRSNDEEE = 9. _____
   Disliked; took exception to for some reason

10. RAMTANOIDI =10. _____
    Respect

11. DPMACLE =11. _____
    Tightly closed

12. BEUUTOIQ =12. _____
    Specialty shop

13. PNAPCHILAAA =13. _____
    Referring to that area of mountains in the eastern U.S.

14. SNIULT =14. _____
    Offend

15. DFIETG =15. _____
    Squirm

Pinballs Vocabulary Juggle Letters 4 Answer Key

1. MICLTMNEOSP = 1. COMPLIMENTS
   To show kindness by a gift

2. VRDHEOE = 2. HOVERED
   Lingered

3. EARDRJ = 3. JARRED
   Bumped

4. ISSINNCOI = 4. INCISIONS
   Cuts

5. PADLEEAP = 5. APPEALED
   Attracted

6. OMCUENM = 6. COMMUNE
   Community where people live and work cooperatively

7. GDLENAR = 7. GNARLED
   Twisted

8. SCINNOOCSU = 8. CONCUSSION
   Swelling from a blow

9. TRSNDEEE = 9. RESENTED
   Disliked; took exception to for some reason

10. RAMTANOIDI =10. ADMIRATION
    Respect

11. DPMACLE =11. CLAMPED
    Tightly closed

12. BEUUTOIQ =12. BOUTIQUE
    Specialty shop

13. PNAPCHILAAA =13. APPALACHIAN
    Referring to that area of mountains in the eastern U.S.

14. SNIULT =14. INSULT
    Offend

15. DFIETG =15. FIDGET
    Squirm

ADMIRATION	Respect
ADOPTIVE	Related by adoption
AGONIZED	Tormented over
APPALACHIAN	Referring to that area of mountains in the eastern U.S.
APPEALED	Attracted
APPENDECTOMY	Operation to remove appendix

ASTONISHED	Shocked
BLURT	Shout
BOUTIQUE	Specialty shop
CLAMPED	Tightly closed
CLENCHED	With jaws tightly closed
COFFIN	Casket; box in which to bury dead person

COMMOTION	Excitement
COMMUNE	Community where people live and work cooperatively
COMPLIMENTS	To show kindness by a gift
CONCUSSION	Swelling from a blow
CONTRACT	Written agreement
DISGUSTED	Repulsed

DREAD	Great fear
EARNESTLY	Sincerely
ESTABLISHED	Founded
FIDGET	Squirm
FORGE	Fake
GNARLED	Twisted

HALTER	Short top that ties behind the neck and across the back
HOVERED	Lingered
HUNCHED	Bent
HYPODERMIC	Needle used under the skin
INCISIONS	Cuts
INSULT	Offend

JARRED	Bumped
MINE	A quarry or well
PITIFUL	Pathetic
REFLECTION	Likeness; mirror image
RESEMBLED	Looked like
RESENTED	Disliked; took exception to for some reason

RESPECTFULLY	Politely
RHYTHMIC	Having a steady motion
SHRIVELED	Withered
SPIGOT	Faucet
SQUINTED	Partly closed eyes; in question
STABILIZES	Calms down

SULKING	Moping
SUMMONED	Called; requested
SUPERIOR	Snobbish; better than others
SUSPICION	Distrust
UNCOMPLIMENTARY	Negative
VACCINES	Preventative shots

VIRUSES	Infections

Pinballs Vocabulary

CONTRACT	ASTONISHED	STABILIZES	BLURT	VIRUSES
HALTER	RESENTED	AGONIZED	APPEALED	ESTABLISHED
COMMOTION	SUSPICION	FREE SPACE	FORGE	INSULT
FIDGET	DREAD	SHRIVELED	RESEMBLED	EARNESTLY
REFLECTION	PITIFUL	BOUTIQUE	SPIGOT	SULKING

Pinballs Vocabulary

COMMUNE	DISGUSTED	VACCINES	CLENCHED	SQUINTED
COFFIN	UNCOMPLIMENTARY	CLAMPED	RESPECTFULLY	CONCUSSION
ADOPTIVE	HOVERED	FREE SPACE	MINE	APPALACHIAN
HYPODERMIC	COMPLIMENTS	JARRED	HUNCHED	APPENDECTOMY
ADMIRATION	SUMMONED	SUPERIOR	INCISIONS	SULKING

Pinballs Vocabulary

APPEALED	UNCOMPLIMENTARY	REFLECTION	SPIGOT	CONCUSSION
HOVERED	APPALACHIAN	COMMUNE	MINE	DREAD
INCISIONS	FORGE	FREE SPACE	BOUTIQUE	CLAMPED
ADOPTIVE	RESEMBLED	JARRED	SHRIVELED	SUSPICION
ESTABLISHED	SUPERIOR	CLENCHED	RESPECTFULLY	COMPLIMENTS

Pinballs Vocabulary

COFFIN	SQUINTED	CONTRACT	ASTONISHED	ADMIRATION
EARNESTLY	COMMOTION	APPENDECTOMY	STABILIZES	GNARLED
SUMMONED	HUNCHED	FREE SPACE	HYPODERMIC	PITIFUL
BLURT	FIDGET	AGONIZED	VIRUSES	VACCINES
HALTER	DISGUSTED	RESENTED	RHYTHMIC	COMPLIMENTS

Pinballs Vocabulary

HYPODERMIC	EARNESTLY	BOUTIQUE	ASTONISHED	JARRED
FIDGET	VIRUSES	ADMIRATION	ESTABLISHED	COFFIN
CONCUSSION	COMMOTION	FREE SPACE	SHRIVELED	SQUINTED
MINE	DISGUSTED	RESENTED	APPALACHIAN	VACCINES
INSULT	CONTRACT	SUPERIOR	SULKING	GNARLED

Pinballs Vocabulary

BLURT	SUMMONED	PITIFUL	UNCOMPLIMENTARY	COMPLIMENTS
SUSPICION	CLAMPED	HUNCHED	COMMUNE	STABILIZES
RESPECTFULLY	HALTER	FREE SPACE	HOVERED	INCISIONS
RESEMBLED	DREAD	SPIGOT	APPEALED	RHYTHMIC
AGONIZED	APPENDECTOMY	ADOPTIVE	FORGE	GNARLED

Pinballs Vocabulary

SULKING	SPIGOT	VIRUSES	HALTER	INSULT
REFLECTION	FIDGET	AGONIZED	SUPERIOR	RESEMBLED
GNARLED	RESPECTFULLY	FREE SPACE	HYPODERMIC	HOVERED
INCISIONS	CLENCHED	ESTABLISHED	BLURT	MINE
SUMMONED	APPEALED	APPALACHIAN	PITIFUL	CONTRACT

Pinballs Vocabulary

EARNESTLY	VACCINES	CLAMPED	UNCOMPLIMENTARY	SQUINTED
BOUTIQUE	SUSPICION	STABILIZES	CONCUSSION	DISGUSTED
JARRED	DREAD	FREE SPACE	SHRIVELED	RHYTHMIC
RESENTED	ADOPTIVE	FORGE	ASTONISHED	COMMUNE
COMMOTION	ADMIRATION	COFFIN	COMPLIMENTS	CONTRACT

Pinballs Vocabulary

BOUTIQUE	CONCUSSION	GNARLED	COMMUNE	EARNESTLY
STABILIZES	SHRIVELED	SUPERIOR	COMPLIMENTS	RESENTED
APPENDECTOMY	COMMOTION	FREE SPACE	HUNCHED	UNCOMPLIMENTARY
HALTER	SUSPICION	CLAMPED	APPALACHIAN	VACCINES
ADMIRATION	SPIGOT	DISGUSTED	CONTRACT	ESTABLISHED

Pinballs Vocabulary

ADOPTIVE	COFFIN	AGONIZED	CLENCHED	VIRUSES
FIDGET	ASTONISHED	JARRED	INCISIONS	INSULT
DREAD	RESPECTFULLY	FREE SPACE	MINE	RHYTHMIC
HYPODERMIC	REFLECTION	PITIFUL	SQUINTED	SUMMONED
APPEALED	BLURT	SULKING	RESEMBLED	ESTABLISHED

Pinballs Vocabulary

COFFIN	JARRED	FORGE	SULKING	ESTABLISHED
AGONIZED	ADMIRATION	FIDGET	HALTER	RESPECTFULLY
BOUTIQUE	SUPERIOR	FREE SPACE	INCISIONS	REFLECTION
SUMMONED	DISGUSTED	STABILIZES	PITIFUL	RESENTED
SHRIVELED	CONCUSSION	COMMOTION	APPENDECTOMY	VIRUSES

Pinballs Vocabulary

RHYTHMIC	BLURT	CLENCHED	ASTONISHED	COMMUNE
SQUINTED	ADOPTIVE	RESEMBLED	CLAMPED	INSULT
APPALACHIAN	HUNCHED	FREE SPACE	UNCOMPLIMENTARY	GNARLED
MINE	SUSPICION	EARNESTLY	CONTRACT	APPEALED
VACCINES	SPIGOT	COMPLIMENTS	HYPODERMIC	VIRUSES

Pinballs Vocabulary

SULKING	COFFIN	INSULT	SUSPICION	AGONIZED
HYPODERMIC	CLENCHED	CONTRACT	VIRUSES	SPIGOT
PITIFUL	REFLECTION	FREE SPACE	CLAMPED	SUPERIOR
COMMUNE	BLURT	MINE	RESEMBLED	HOVERED
ADMIRATION	FORGE	JARRED	STABILIZES	SUMMONED

Pinballs Vocabulary

APPENDECTOMY	VACCINES	DREAD	COMMOTION	ASTONISHED
INCISIONS	APPALACHIAN	DISGUSTED	RESPECTFULLY	SQUINTED
BOUTIQUE	UNCOMPLIMENTARY	FREE SPACE	HUNCHED	ESTABLISHED
APPEALED	RESENTED	GNARLED	HALTER	FIDGET
RHYTHMIC	COMPLIMENTS	ADOPTIVE	CONCUSSION	SUMMONED

Pinballs Vocabulary

RHYTHMIC	DREAD	APPALACHIAN	COMMUNE	HUNCHED
ADMIRATION	COFFIN	GNARLED	AGONIZED	DISGUSTED
APPEALED	FORGE	FREE SPACE	SUPERIOR	CONTRACT
COMMOTION	ADOPTIVE	FIDGET	INSULT	INCISIONS
CLENCHED	EARNESTLY	CONCUSSION	SUSPICION	RESENTED

Pinballs Vocabulary

RESEMBLED	ASTONISHED	CLAMPED	SHRIVELED	BLURT
MINE	HALTER	UNCOMPLIMENTARY	SULKING	HOVERED
RESPECTFULLY	HYPODERMIC	FREE SPACE	VIRUSES	APPENDECTOMY
SUMMONED	VACCINES	SPIGOT	JARRED	SQUINTED
REFLECTION	COMPLIMENTS	PITIFUL	STABILIZES	RESENTED

Pinballs Vocabulary

COFFIN	HALTER	CLENCHED	INCISIONS	ADOPTIVE
APPALACHIAN	SPIGOT	SUMMONED	RESEMBLED	SQUINTED
SHRIVELED	ADMIRATION	FREE SPACE	EARNESTLY	REFLECTION
COMMUNE	INSULT	CLAMPED	GNARLED	ESTABLISHED
SUPERIOR	ASTONISHED	COMPLIMENTS	VACCINES	STABILIZES

Pinballs Vocabulary

APPEALED	FORGE	CONCUSSION	BOUTIQUE	HUNCHED
AGONIZED	COMMOTION	PITIFUL	CONTRACT	JARRED
RESPECTFULLY	FIDGET	FREE SPACE	SULKING	DREAD
UNCOMPLIMENTARY	DISGUSTED	VIRUSES	SUSPICION	BLURT
HOVERED	HYPODERMIC	MINE	RHYTHMIC	STABILIZES

Pinballs Vocabulary

FORGE	SHRIVELED	HOVERED	CLAMPED	GNARLED
ADMIRATION	EARNESTLY	ADOPTIVE	CLENCHED	APPENDECTOMY
CONTRACT	CONCUSSION	FREE SPACE	BLURT	SULKING
JARRED	FIDGET	STABILIZES	SPIGOT	COFFIN
DREAD	DISGUSTED	RESENTED	MINE	BOUTIQUE

Pinballs Vocabulary

UNCOMPLIMENTARY	COMMUNE	AGONIZED	ASTONISHED	COMMOTION
INSULT	HYPODERMIC	VIRUSES	PITIFUL	SUMMONED
RHYTHMIC	HALTER	FREE SPACE	COMPLIMENTS	ESTABLISHED
RESPECTFULLY	INCISIONS	VACCINES	SUPERIOR	APPALACHIAN
REFLECTION	HUNCHED	SQUINTED	SUSPICION	BOUTIQUE

Pinballs Vocabulary

FORGE	SHRIVELED	SPIGOT	RESPECTFULLY	ADMIRATION
CONCUSSION	JARRED	RHYTHMIC	HALTER	ASTONISHED
VIRUSES	APPALACHIAN	FREE SPACE	SUPERIOR	ESTABLISHED
HYPODERMIC	SQUINTED	UNCOMPLIMENTARY	EARNESTLY	VACCINES
RESEMBLED	CONTRACT	CLAMPED	PITIFUL	BOUTIQUE

Pinballs Vocabulary

DREAD	APPEALED	COFFIN	COMMOTION	DISGUSTED
INSULT	STABILIZES	APPENDECTOMY	FIDGET	INCISIONS
SULKING	RESENTED	FREE SPACE	SUSPICION	COMMUNE
COMPLIMENTS	MINE	CLENCHED	HUNCHED	ADOPTIVE
SUMMONED	BLURT	HOVERED	AGONIZED	BOUTIQUE

Pinballs Vocabulary

BOUTIQUE	APPALACHIAN	INSULT	MINE	HUNCHED
RESEMBLED	VACCINES	SUMMONED	REFLECTION	SPIGOT
JARRED	FORGE	FREE SPACE	INCISIONS	CONCUSSION
DISGUSTED	GNARLED	HYPODERMIC	PITIFUL	BLURT
ASTONISHED	SHRIVELED	VIRUSES	APPENDECTOMY	HOVERED

Pinballs Vocabulary

SUSPICION	COMMUNE	HALTER	RESENTED	EARNESTLY
SQUINTED	UNCOMPLIMENTARY	CLAMPED	ESTABLISHED	RHYTHMIC
SUPERIOR	CONTRACT	FREE SPACE	RESPECTFULLY	ADMIRATION
ADOPTIVE	SULKING	AGONIZED	COFFIN	CLENCHED
STABILIZES	COMMOTION	APPEALED	DREAD	HOVERED

Pinballs Vocabulary

RESPECTFULLY	EARNESTLY	STABILIZES	APPEALED	APPALACHIAN
RESEMBLED	MINE	HALTER	SPIGOT	DREAD
PITIFUL	CONTRACT	FREE SPACE	INSULT	APPENDECTOMY
CONCUSSION	BLURT	FIDGET	SUPERIOR	CLENCHED
ADOPTIVE	DISGUSTED	CLAMPED	COFFIN	HYPODERMIC

Pinballs Vocabulary

HOVERED	COMPLIMENTS	SQUINTED	REFLECTION	FORGE
HUNCHED	ASTONISHED	COMMUNE	ESTABLISHED	GNARLED
ADMIRATION	AGONIZED	FREE SPACE	RHYTHMIC	UNCOMPLIMENTARY
VIRUSES	RESENTED	INCISIONS	SUSPICION	VACCINES
SHRIVELED	SUMMONED	COMMOTION	SULKING	HYPODERMIC

Pinballs Vocabulary

VIRUSES	APPALACHIAN	COMMOTION	DISGUSTED	PITIFUL
RESPECTFULLY	HYPODERMIC	REFLECTION	COMPLIMENTS	GNARLED
RESENTED	MINE	FREE SPACE	ESTABLISHED	JARRED
RESEMBLED	DREAD	SUSPICION	INSULT	HOVERED
SQUINTED	SHRIVELED	BLURT	FORGE	SUMMONED

Pinballs Vocabulary

SPIGOT	AGONIZED	ADMIRATION	VACCINES	SULKING
ASTONISHED	CONTRACT	EARNESTLY	APPEALED	CONCUSSION
COFFIN	APPENDECTOMY	FREE SPACE	STABILIZES	INCISIONS
HALTER	COMMUNE	BOUTIQUE	FIDGET	CLENCHED
ADOPTIVE	HUNCHED	CLAMPED	UNCOMPLIMENTARY	SUMMONED

Pinballs Vocabulary

PITIFUL	COMMOTION	SUSPICION	CONCUSSION	ADMIRATION
DREAD	APPENDECTOMY	FORGE	RESEMBLED	REFLECTION
JARRED	FIDGET	FREE SPACE	STABILIZES	RESPECTFULLY
AGONIZED	HYPODERMIC	SUMMONED	DISGUSTED	BOUTIQUE
ADOPTIVE	UNCOMPLIMENTARY	APPALACHIAN	RESENTED	CONTRACT

Pinballs Vocabulary

SPIGOT	CLAMPED	ESTABLISHED	VIRUSES	SHRIVELED
HOVERED	GNARLED	RHYTHMIC	ASTONISHED	SULKING
INCISIONS	CLENCHED	FREE SPACE	COMPLIMENTS	MINE
COFFIN	SUPERIOR	BLURT	EARNESTLY	APPEALED
COMMUNE	SQUINTED	HUNCHED	INSULT	CONTRACT

Pinballs Vocabulary

CLAMPED	APPALACHIAN	BOUTIQUE	DISGUSTED	HUNCHED
CLENCHED	STABILIZES	SHRIVELED	ESTABLISHED	HOVERED
FIDGET	SUMMONED	FREE SPACE	MINE	APPEALED
VIRUSES	HYPODERMIC	APPENDECTOMY	SUSPICION	HALTER
COFFIN	UNCOMPLIMENTARY	COMMUNE	INSULT	DREAD

Pinballs Vocabulary

RESPECTFULLY	ADOPTIVE	GNARLED	RESENTED	FORGE
COMPLIMENTS	CONTRACT	SUPERIOR	INCISIONS	COMMOTION
REFLECTION	EARNESTLY	FREE SPACE	CONCUSSION	ADMIRATION
ASTONISHED	SPIGOT	RESEMBLED	BLURT	JARRED
SQUINTED	AGONIZED	SULKING	RHYTHMIC	DREAD